Frederic William Farrar

Eternal Hope

Five Sermons Preached in Westminster Abbey, November and December, 1877

Frederic William Farrar

Eternal Hope
Five Sermons Preached in Westminster Abbey, November and December, 1877

ISBN/EAN: 9783337085926

Printed in Europe, USA, Canada, Australia, Japan

Cover: Foto ©Lupo / pixelio.de

More available books at **www.hansebooks.com**

ETERNAL HOPE

Five Sermons

PREACHED IN WESTMINSTER ABBEY,
NOVEMBER AND DECEMBER, 1877

BY THE

REV. FREDERIC W. FARRAR, D.D., F.R.S.,

Canon of Westminster,

Chaplain in Ordinary to the Queen,

*Late Master of Marlborough College, Hulsean Lecturer, and Fellow of
Trinity College, Cambridge*

" Plerique dum plus nos diligunt quam meremur, haec jactant et loquuntur,
sermones nostris doctrinamque laudantes, quae conscientia nostra non recipit.
Alii vero tractatus nostros calumniantes ca sentire nos criminantur quae
nunquam sensisse nos novimus."—ORIGEN, *Homil.* xxv. in Luc.

NEW YORK
E. P. DUTTON & COMPANY
1878

New York : J. J. Little & Co., Printers,
10 to 20 Astor Place.

"Oh remember how short my time is :
Wherefore hast thou made all men for nought ?"

Ps. lxxxix. 48.

" τοιοῖδε μόχθου τέρμα μή τι προσδόκα,
πρὶν ἂν θεῶν τις διάδοχος τῶν σῶν πόνων
φανῇ, θελήσῃ τ' εἰς ἀναύγητον μολεῖν
Ἅιδην κνεφαῖά τ' ἀμφὶ Ταρτάρου βάθη.
πρὸς ταῦτα βούλευ'."

ÆSCH. *Prom.* v. 1026.

" Δίφιλος ὁ κώμικος τοιαῦτά τινα περὶ τῆς κρίσεως διαλέγεται,
καὶ γὰρ καθ' Ἅιδην δύο τρίβους νομίζομεν
μίαν δικαίων χἀτέραν ἀσεβῶν ὁδόν
  *   *   *   *   *
συνᾴδει δὲ τούτοις ἡ τραγῳδία . . .
ἐπὰν δ' ἄρ' ἐκλίπῃ τὸ πᾶν
φροῦδος μὲν ἔσται κυμάτων ἅπας βυθός . . .
κἄπειτα σώσει πάνθ' ἃ προσθ' ἀπώλεσεν."

CLEM. ALEX. *Strom.* v. 14, § 123.

" Facta resurrectione mortuorum *non deerunt quibus* post poenas, quas patiuntur spiritus mortuorum, impertiatur misericordia, ut in ignem non mittantur aeternum."—AUG. *De Civ. Dei*, xxi. 24.

" Deus non exigit ab ullo peccatore plus quam debet, sed quoniam nullus potest reddere quantum debet, solus Christus reddidit pro omnibus plus quam debetur."—ST. ANSELM.

" Esto cavernoso, quia sic pro labe necesse est
    Corporeâ, tristis me sorbeat ignis averno,
    Saltem mirificos incendia lenta vapores
    Exhalent, aestuque calor languente tepescat.
    Lux immensa alios et tempora vincta coronis
    Laetificent, me poena levis clementer adurat."
                    PRUDENT. *Hamartigeneia, ad fin.*

" E vederai color, che son contenti
    Nel fuoco, perchè speran di venire
    Quando che sia, alle beate genti."
                    DANTE, *Inferno*, i. 118.

" Through sins of sense, perversities of will,
    Through doubt and pain, through guilt and shame, and ill
    Thy pitying Eye is on Thy creature still.

" Wilt Thou not make, eternal Source and Goal !
    In Thy long years life's broken circle whole,
    And change to praise the cry of a lost soul?"

" Wilt thou draw near the nature of the gods ?
    Draw near them then in being merciful !"

" Let no one take offence at the opening of this mystery as though it brought anything new into religion ; for it has nothing new in it ; it alters no point of gospel doctrine, but only sets each article of the old Christian faith upon its true ground."—W. LAW, *Way to Divine Knowledge*, p. 255.

" Rabbi Ishmael Ben Elisha said, Once, I entered into the Holy of Holies [as High Priest] to burn incense, when I saw Aktriel [the Divine Crown] Jah, Lord of Hosts, sitting upon a throne, high and lifted up, who said unto me, ' Ishmael, my son, bless me.' I answered, ' *May it please Thee to make Thy compassion prevail over Thine anger ; may it be revealed above Thy other attributes ; mayest Thou deal with Thy children according to it, and not according to the strict measure of judgment.*' It seemed to me that He bowed His head, as though to answer Amen to my blessing."—*Talmud* (Bera-chôth, i. f. 6. b.)

" St. John uses a very broad expression. ' Jesus Christ,' he says, ' is the propitiation for our sins, and not for ours only, but also *for the sins of the whole world.*' ' The whole world.'—' Ah ! ' some would say, ' that is dangerous language.' It is God's language— John speaking as he was moved by the Holy Ghost. It throws a zone of mercy around the world. Perish the hand that would narrow it by a hairsbreadth."— REV. DR. GUTHRIE, *Life*, p. 511.

" My belief is that in the end there will be a vastly larger number saved than we have any conception of. What sort of earthly govern-ment would that be where more than half the subjects were in prison ? I cannot believe that the government of God will be like that."—*Id.* p. 773.

PREFACE.

THE complaint of Origen as to the misrepresentation of his real views alike by friends and opponents, which stands on the title-page of this volume, will exactly express my reason for publishing it. Most unexpectedly, most reluctantly, I find myself entangled in a controversy into which I should not have voluntarily entered without buckling on armour of stronger temper and securer rivets than I can, at this sudden call, find ready to hand. These sermons were never intended for publication. They were preached in the ordinary course of my duties, and I refused multitudes of requests to give them a wider publicity, until it became necessary to do so in simple self-defence against the many perversions of my real views, which were prevalent among those who had not heard the sermons,

or those who reported them imperfectly and erroneously. The notes and appendices were not prepared
beforehand, but written in the very brief and incessantly occupied space of time which intervened
between my decision to publish them and their actual
appearance.[1] Of the truths here propounded I have
never since my early youth had the slightest doubt; but
had I intended any controversial defence of them, it
would have been far fuller and more impregnable than I
now can make it. If, in mere collateral matters, I have
made any slips, the candid reader (and to such only I

---

[1] In drawing them up I have received some assistance from books
which have since been kindly sent me, mostly by their authors,
but not one of which I had previously read. Of the arguments of
these writers I have made little or no use, but I have borrowed
some of their quotations. Among these I may mention especially
Mr. Jukes's *Restitution of All Things*, a singularly calm, devout,
and thoughtful treatise; Dr. Dewes's *Plea for a Rational Translation*; the Rev. H. N. Oxenham's *Catholic Eschatology*; and
the Rev. C. Clemance's *Future Punishment*. The Rev. S. Minton
kindly sent me his *Glory of Christ*, and other publications; the Rev.
E. White his *Life in Christ*; and I have also had lent to me
The Perishing Soul, by Mr. Dennistoun; the Rev. Prebendary
Constable's *Duration of Future Punishment*; and numerous
pamphlets, for which my best thanks are due to the authors.

appeal) will make every allowance for one who, amid many occupations, has been unexpectedly called upon to defend opinions which have been incessantly assailed, but which, in the only form in which he holds them, he believes to be not only tenable and permissible—(this they are beyond all question)—but to be also Scriptural, necessary, and true. In a very high sense also he believes them to be Catholic. An 'opinion' indeed, can never be 'Catholic' in the same sense as a matter of faith ; but my views on the subject are in agreement with Catholic theology—both before and after the Reformation—to an extent of which I believe that few are aware. And this will I hope appear when I have endeavoured to state with all possible clearness what my opinions really are.

Among innumerable varieties of detail into which it is impossible to enter, it may be said that four main views of Eschatology are now prevalent, namely—

1. *Universalism*, or, as it is now sometimes termed Restorationism : the opinion that all men will be ultimately saved.

2. *Annihilationism*, or, as its supporters prefer to

call it, "conditional immortality:" the opinion that after a retributive punishment the wicked will be destroyed.

3. *Purgatory,*—the view that besides Heaven, the final state of the blessed, and Hell, the final doom of the accursed, there is a state wherein those souls are detained and punished which are capable of being purified,—an intermediate purification between death and judgment.

4. The *Common* view, which, to the utter detriment of all noble thoughts of God, and to all joy and peace in believing, except in the case of many who shut their eyes hard to what it really implies— declares (i.) that at death there is passed upon every impenitent sinner an irreversible doom to endless tortures, either material or mental, of the most awful and unspeakable intensity; and (ii.) that this doom awaits the vast majority of mankind. If this be not the ordinary view, it were well that it should be explicitly disclaimed. It most certainly is the view which has been crudely inculcated from multitudes of pulpits, even in the last few months.

Let me speak very briefly on each of these views in order.

1. The strength of *Universalism* lies in two arguments ; those, namely, which are derived (1) from our belief in the infinite love of God,—in that divine mercy which is from everlasting to everlasting ; and (2) from the very numerous passages of Scripture which speak repeatedly, and without any limitation, of the Restoration of all things and the Universality of Christian Redemption.

Every man must long with all his heart that this belief were true ; and thousands have repeated with intense yearning the famous lines of the poet of *In Memoriam*—

> " Oh yet we trust that somehow good
>   Shall be the final end of ill,
>   To pangs of nature, sins of will,
> Defects of doubt, and taints of blood ;

> " That nothing walks with aimless feet ;
>   That not one life shall be destroy'd,
>   Or cast as rubbish in the void,
> When God hath made the pile complete."

But however deep may be our desire that this should be the will of God; however beautifully it may seem to accord both with His mercy and His justice, that sin, after bringing its own punishment, should be turned to holiness, and so forgiven; however much we may cling to the hope that some such meaning may under-lie the broad and boundless promises of a future Restitution,—I dare not lay down any dogma of Universalism; partly because it is not clearly revealed to us, and partly because it is impossible for us to estimate the hardening effect of obstinate persistence in evil, and the power of the human will to resist the law and reject the love of God.

2. Nor can I at all accept the theory of Conditional Irmoriality. Ably and earnestly as good men have argued in its favour, it seems to me to rest too entirely on the supposed invariable meaning of a few words, and to press that meaning too far; it rejects that instinctive belief in Immortality which has been found in almost every age and every race of man; and while it relieves the soul from the crushing horror involved in the conception of endless

torment, it still—if I understand it right—leaves us with the ghastly conclusion that God will raise the wicked from the dead only that they may be tormented and at last destroyed.[1]

3. Nor again can I accept the Roman doctrine of *Purgatory.* If indeed that doctrine consisted in nothing else but these words from the catechism of the Council of Trent, that "there is a purgatorial fire where the souls of the righteous are purified by punishment of some fixed period, that entrance may be given them into their eternal home, where nothing that is defiled can have a place,"—and if the term "fire" may be interpreted immaterially, as the Eastern Church and Western theologians of all ages have decided that it

[1] For Mr. E. White, Mr. Minton, Prebendary Constable, and the other members of this school of thought, I feel a sincere respect ; but with them, as with others, it seems to me that " the letter killeth." Rigid literalism is absolutely fatal to any true knowledge of Scripture. The highest service these truly devout, earnest, and able writers have done is to point out the utter untenability of the popular view. Their view is far more scriptural, as well as incomparably less shocking, than the utterances of those who defend the traditional fancies,—whether the latter be hard and illiterate, or learned and refined.

b

may,[1] then there would be nothing in the doctrine of Purgatory which seems to me in any way inconsistent with Scripture, while it certainly is consistent with a very ancient belief of the Church, and with the all but universal usage of prayers for the dead.[2] Had this been the whole Roman doctrine of Purgatory, I do not believe that the Reformers would ever have stigmatised it as "*res futilis.*" But they rejected it in the rough, not only because the conception had been made too compact, too specific, too much limited to the *poena temporalis*, in short, too systematic, to be capable of exact Scriptural proof; but also because it was connected in their minds with the deplorable but parasitic abuses of indulgences, pardons, works of supererogation, purchasable masses for the dead, and all the sixteenth century devices of Tetzel and Leo X.

---

[1] "Poenam ignis, sive iste ignis accipiatur proprie sive metaphorice," Bellarmine, *Purg.* ii. 10. "Why should the 'fire of hell' be more material than the 'water of life'? Why should the 'furnace' and 'lake' of Gehenna possess more of physical reality than 'the sea of glass' or the 'pearly gates'?"

[2] The Catacombs furnish decisive proof of the antiquity of this practice.

But as I have intimated elsewhere (see pp. 169—174), it was a deep misfortune to the Church that, while rejecting Purgatory, the Reformers did not distinguish it from the widespread ancient, reasonable, and, I had almost said, necessary, belief in some condition in which —by what means we know not, whether by the *poena sensûs* or only the *poena damni*—imperfect souls who die in a state unfit for heaven may yet have perfected in them until the day of Christ, that good work of God which has been in this world begun.[1] There are few great theologians, whether of pre-Reformation or of modern times, who have not used language which, consciously or unconsciously, favours such a view as this.

I do not then by any means hold the "Romish doctrine of Purgatory" in the dogmatic and corrupted form in which it is distinctly and rightly condemned by the Twenty-second Article. But this "Roman doctrine," thus stated, is not to be confused with the opinion of many of the Fathers that there is *some* intermediate

---

[1] Phil. i. 6. See Oxenham's *Catholic Eschatology*, and a thoughtful article on "The Annihilation of the Wicked" in the *Church Quarterly*, of July 1877.

state wherein souls which, at the time of death, are
still imperfect and unworthy, and not yet in a state
of grace—and of such are the vast majority of us all
—may still be reached by God's mercy beyond the
grave. The learned and thoughtful Lutheran Bishop
Martensen, after arguing in favour of "a realm of progressive development in which souls are prepared and
matured for the final judgment," adds that though the
Romish doctrine "must be repudiated because it is
mixed up with so many crude and false positions, it
nevertheless contains the truth that the intermediate
state must, in a purely spiritual sense, be a Purgatory
destined for the purifying of the soul."[1]   I so far differ
from him that I think the term "Purgatory" had
better be rejected, not because we are averse to the
acceptance of such truths as the word involves, from
whatever quarter they may come to us, but because it
is inextricably mixed up with a number of views in
which we cannot at all believe.[2]

[1] *Christian Dogmatics*, p. 457, E. Tr.
[2] On this unfortunate *negativeness* in the teaching of the Reformers
upon this subject, see the Sketch of Eschatological Opinions, p. 181.

4. And now I come to the common, the popular view in our own Church.

It is of course absolutely false that in any one of the following sermons—as some declare that we say, and as we be slanderously reported—I have ever dreamt of denying the great, awful, but neither unjust nor unmerciful doctrine of future retribution. The statements which have been so freely circulated in England and in America that I "denied the existence of hell," or "denounced the doctrine of eternal punishment," are merely ignorant perversions of what I tried to teach.[1]

---

[1] Mr. Clemance, in whose little book I find much with which I can agree, argues that future punishment may *end*, but that the ending is unrevealed. While, therefore, he would not teach that it *must* end, neither can he teach that it will *not*. "All that God is in Himself, all that He is known to be to me through this revelation of Himself in Christ Jesus, give us an infinite satisfaction in leaving the matter with Him If we affirm *annihilation* we distort Scripture ; if we affirm *universalism* we oppose Scripture ; if we affirm the ending of punishment we fall short of Scripture ; *if we affirm its endlessness, we go beyond Scripture.*" P. 80. I would go a little further than Mr. Clemance in expressing a distinct *hope*, and I do not think that he gives due weight to the doctrine of the ἐποκατάστασις πάντων.

Between me and the great majority of our most learned clergy and theologians,—between my view and that of many of our wisest and most respected bishops, —the differences are very small; and only lie within that range of opinions in which such differences are absolutely permissible.   Neither the Catholic Church in general, nor the English branch of it in particular, has ever condemned the view which I here have preached.[1] That it is not, and never has been the opinion of the numerical majority I am well aware, but that it is, openly, or more often tacitly, accepted by an ever-increasing number of our most thoughtful and educated living divines I have the best reason to believe ; and that it will be the professed and deeply-treasured belief of another generation of the English clergy, I am most unalterably convinced.

That there is a terrible retribution upon impenitent sin both here and hereafter ; that without holiness no

---

[1] I say "has ever condemned," for though I think that the English Church showed the highest wisdom in rejecting the Forty-second Article, yet it contains nothing in which (if I understand it rightly) I should refuse to concur.

man can ever see the Lord ; that sin cannot be forgiven till it is forsaken and repented of ; that the doom, which falls on sin is both merciful and just—we are all agreed : and these views will be found enforced in the following pages. If this be all that is generally intended by the doctrine of Hell,—as it is most assuredly all that the Catholic Church, guided by Scripture, requires her children to believe—then *this* doctrine of Hell I receive and believe. But there are four elements in the current opinion which I consider to be as unsupported by Scripture as they are repugnant to reason ;—which are matters of opinion only and not of faith ;—which the Church of God has never dogmatically sanctioned ;—which have furnished to the atheist his most indisputable argument, and caused to the Christian—if he be a thoughtful Christian—his most intolerable pang. It is these accretions of the true doctrine, and these only, which I have shown reasons to repudiate and condemn. These four elements— which make the popular view far darker than that held in the Roman Church, and far darker even than that of St. Augustine—are I, the physical torments, the material agonies, the "*sapiens ignis*" of Eternal Punishment;[1] 2, the supposition of its necessarily endless duration for all who incur it; 3, the opinion that it is thus incurred by the vast mass of mankind; and 4, that it is a doom passed irreversibly at the moment of death on all who die in a state of sin. How frightful are the facts which *they* must face who hold these common opinions—if indeed they in any way realise the meaning of their own words —is obvious to all, and I have given some proofs of it in their own words. How any man with a heart of pity in him—any man who has the faculty of imagination in even the lowest degree developed—can contemplate the present condition of countless multitudes of the dead and of the living viewed in the light of such opinions;—how he can at all reconcile them either with all that he learns of God and of Christ in Scripture and by inward experience,—how

---

[1] Minuc. Felix, *Oct.* 35. "Illic sapiens ignis membra urit et reficit, carpit et nutrit." "In bodily awful, intolerable torture we believe no longer. At the idea of a *bodily* hell we have learnt to smile." F. W. Robertson. (I cannot endorse this expression.)

—as he walks the streets and witnesses the life of our great cities—he can enjoy in this world one moment of happiness however deeply he may be convinced of his own individual salvation—is more than I can ever understand. And it is really painful to think that in this matter the Roman Catholic Church, so rigidly tenacious of what she conceives to be purity of doctrine, so intensely opposed to anything remotely resembling the spirit of scepticism, so inflexibly resolute in opposition to heresies, so rich in her motherhood of saintly souls, has held a doctrine more merciful, less void of pity, than the current belief of modern Protestants. That doctrine the Romanists have held—though they have overlaid it with many untenable inferences—because they inherited it from the early Church. Those who uphold the popular view in all its tetanic rigidity accuse others of looking lightly at sin. Will the most fanatical bigot say that the Roman Church takes a light view of sin? yet that Church has introduced an almost indefinite alleviation into the belief in an endless hell!

Restore the ancient belief in an intermediate state;

—correct the glaring and most unhappy mistranslations of our English version;—judge the words of our Blessed Lord by the most ordinary rules of honest and unprejudiced interpretation;—abstain from pressing the literal acceptance of passages most obviously metaphorical;[1]—give due weight to the countless passages of Scripture, from Genesis to Revelation, which speak of a love, and a mercy, and a triumph of long-sufferring over offended justice, which are to us irreconcilable with the belief that the unhappy race of God's children in this great family of man are all but universally doomed to endless torturings, at the very thought of which the heart faints and is sick with horror;—give to the Reason and the Conscience,[2] of man some voice in judging of a scheme which seems to outrage all that is noblest and holiest within them;—separate from the notions of "Hell" (if the word be restored to its ancient sense) the arbitrary

---

[1] Es ist offenbar dass viele Ausdrücke des Neuen Testaments, welche dieser äusserlichen Zustand Z. B. als ein ewig brennendes Feuer bezeichnen (Matt. xxv. 41) *nur bildlich zu nehmen sind.*" Märtens *Ersch. u. Grüber, s. v.*   [2] 2 Cor. iv, 3.

fancies of human ignorance and human passion ;—
accept the merciful opinions which the Church has
always permitted though she has not formally adopted
them—that the fire of Gehenna is metaphorical,—that
there is a possibility of future purification—that most
men will at last be saved ; [1]—hold that, as the very
word "damnation" once implied, the *poena damni*,—
i.e. the loss, it may be for ever, of the beatific vision—
is, far more than any *poena sensûs*, or physical torture,
the essence of the sufferings of the lost ;—do this, and
you have removed the greatest of all stumbling-blocks
from the path of faith, and added incomparably to our
love of God and to the peace, the hope, the dignity,
the happiness of human life.

---

[1] On these points as permissible in the Roman Church, see
Perrone, *Pracl. Theol.* i. 484. The latter was held by F. W. Faber
(*Creator and Creature*, iii. 332 : "In the use of the Scripture argument
the triumph is completely and most remarkably on the milder side"),
and the eloquent Lacordaire. H. N. Oxenham, *Eschatology*, p. 59.
He calls some of the vulgar opinions "parasitical accretions . . . .
as startling and repulsive as they are destitute of any reasonable or
authoritative basis," and "matters of speculation on which in all
ages different opinions have been maintained by theologians of
unimpeached orthodoxy."

Now my objection to the renderings of Γέεννα, κρίσις, and αἰώνιος, by "hell," "damnation," and "everlasting" —an objection in accordance with the instinctive feeling of thousands, as is obvious from the universal practice of avoiding those words—arises from these grounds :— that as English words they have utterly lost their original significance ; that by nine hundred and ninety-nine out of every thousand they are understood in a sense which I see to be demonstrably unscriptural and untrue ; and that they attribute to the sacred writers, and to our Blessed Lord Himself, meanings such as they never sanctioned, language such as they never used. Not one of them can be retained by our revisers without necessitating hereafter yet another revision. I would say this very humbly, but I cannot state it too strongly. It is a matter not of opinion but of fact. Whether men hold the doctrine of an irreversible doom to endless torments passed at death on all who die unforgiven or not, is not a question which can in any way affect the demonstrable meaning of Greek words,—the undeniable duty of giving to those words such renderings only as do not stereotype foregone conclusions in matters of immemorial controversy.

I know that inveterate prejudice, passing into second habit by centuries of tyrannous tradition, is invincible in all but the noblest souls. The roots of the mandrake were believed to strike very deeply into the soil, and when it was torn up it shrieked. Yet let every candid reader perpend these simple, undeniable, and indisputable facts.

1. The verb "to damn" and its cognates does not once occur in the Old Testament.

No word conveying any such meaning occurs in the Greek of the New Testament.

The words so rendered mean "to judge," "judgment," and "condemnation"; and if the word "damnation" has come to mean *more* than these words do—as, to all but the most educated readers, is notoriously the case—then the word is a grievous mistranslation, all the more serious because it entirely and terribly perverts and obscures the real meaning of our Lord's utterances ; and all the more inexcusable, at any rate for us with our present knowledge, because if the word "damnation" were used as the rendering of the very same words in multitudes of other passages (where our translators have rightly translated them), it would make those passages at once impossible and grotesque.[1]

2. The word "*Hell*," in the Old Testament represents the single word *Sheôl* (שְׁאוֹל), which means neither more nor less than "the unseen world," or "the world beyond the grave," and is in thirty-three places rendered "the grave."[2]

In the New Testament it is used to render three words, neither of which conveys, or could have been originally intended to convey, the notion which all but the few now attach to "hell." Now if a word conveys meanings which are not necessarily involved in the original, it is an inadequate translation; if it conveys to the vast majority meanings which have nothing

---

[1] The gratuitous introduction of "damnation" for "judgment" into 1 Cor. xi. 29, and so into our Communion Service, has been a *sad* cause of spiritual loss to thousands of timid souls.

[2] The word has in fact changed its meanings. It once meant (as is shown alike by our own and by Luther's version) merely "the underworld"; it has now *come to mean* a place of endless torment. See Ersch and Grüber *s. v.*, Hölle, and Excursus II. p. 195.

corresponding to them in the original, it is a mistranslation ; if it be deliberately retained after it has acquired a shade of meaning far darker than the original, and far darker than formerly belonged to it, is it too much to say that it will be a mistranslation which a multitude of readers will find it very hard to condone ?

a. One of the three words rendered " hell " occurs but once, in 2 Pet. ii. 4. It is the Greek *Tartarus*, and ought to be so rendered. It cannot be rendered " hell," for it refers to an intermediate state previous to judgment.

β. Another is *Hades*, which is the exact equivalent of the Hebrew *Sheôl*, and means " the unseen world," as a place both for the bad and the good (Acts ii. 27, 36). It tells directly against the received notion of " hell," because (like Tartarus in 2 Pet. ii. 4), it means an intermediate state of the soul previous to judgment.[1]

---

[1] This is the word used in Luke xvi. 23 of Dives.—" In Hades he lift up his eyes being in torments." So far therefore from furnishing any argument in favour of the popular view, this parable tells distinctly against it, since it points to an intermediate condition—as Stier admits (*Words of the Lord Jesus*, iv. 223, E. Tr.) ;—and it shows how rapidly in that condition a moral renovation has been

γ. A third is *Gehenna*. It is most essential that this word should be rightly understood, because (with the exception of James iii. 6—a mere incidental allusion in no wise bearing on the history of the word) it is used by our Lord alone.

In the Old Testament it is merely the pleasant Valley of Hinnom (Ge Hinnom), subsequently desecrated by idolatry, and specially by Moloch worship, and defiled by Josiah on this account.[1] Used, according to Jewish tradition, as the common sewer of the city, the corpses of the worse criminals were flung into it unburied, and fires were lit to purify the contaminated air. It then became a word which secondarily implied (i) the severest judgment which a Jewish court could pass

wrought in a sinful and selfish soul (see some excellent remarks in Mr. Cox's *Salvator Mundi*, p. 65). Neander goes perhaps too far in saying that it is foreign to the scope of the parable to give us any clue to the future life ; but the expression "*Abraham's bosom*" shows how utterly figurative it is, and Stier holds that the βα'σανοι were meant to work repentance. Even Luther, Von Gerlach, &c., teach that " the whole conversation passed in the conscience." And Dives is τέκνον still.

[1] See 1 Kings xi. 7 ; 2 Kings xxiii. 10 (Jer. vii. 31, xix. 10--14 ; Is. xxx. 33, Tophet)

upon a criminal—the casting forth of his unburied corpse amid the fires and worms of this polluted valley ; and (ii.) a punishment—which to the Jews, as a body—*never* meant an endless punishment beyond the grave.[1]

Whatever may be the meaning of the entire passages in which this word occurs, "hell" must be a complete mistranslation, since it attributes to the term used by Christ a sense entirely different from that in which it was understood by our Lord's hearers, and therefore entirely different from the sense in which He could have used it. I must not shrink from recording my most emphatic opinion that if the Revision

---

[1] Schleusner (*Lex N. T. s. v.*), though holding the traditional view without any suspicion of its utter groundlessness, yet renders Matt. v. 22, ἔνοχος ἔσται εἰς τὴν γέενναν τοῦ πυρός by "*dignus qui contumeliosâ morte afficiatur.*" If any one will give one moment's unbiassed thought to this verse, so obviously figurative—since in its literal sense it was of course not the case that angry thoughts, or common expletives came under the cognizance of the Jewish courts, and since it is utterly shocking to the moral sense to suppose that an angry word will doom men to endless torment—he will see how utterly the sense is *travestied* by the introduction of hell-fire for "the Gehenna of fire," into the English version.

Committee retain the word "hell" as a correct version of Gehenna they will be incurring a very grave and awful responsibility, by perpetuating a connotation for which, long after they are in the grave, they will be condemned by the next generation far more unsparingly than by our own.

3. I now come to αἰώνιος, translated rightly and frequently by "eternal," and wrongly and unnecessarily by "everlasting."

I say wrongly on grounds which cannot be impeached. If in numbers of passages this word confessedly does not and *cannot* mean "endless,"[1]—a fact which none but the grossest and most hopeless

---

[1] See for αἰώνιος Is. lviii. 12; Jer. li. 39; Gen. ix. 12, xvii. 8, xlviii. 2, xlix. 26; Num. xxv. 13; Lev. iii. 17, xvi. 34; Hab. iii. 6; and for αἰών Deut. xiii. 16, xv. 17; Eccl. xii. 5; Ex. xxxii. 13; 2 Kings v. 27, xxi. 7; 1 Chron. xxviii. 4; Rom. xvi. 25; 2 Tim. i. 9; Tit. i. 2; &c. &c. It is remarkable further that the expressions of the duration of good are *far* stronger than any that are applied to evil (Is. li. 6—8; Ps. cxlv. 13; Eph. iii. 21); also that the expression "eternal death" occurs nowhere in Scripture. He who said αἰώνιον πῦρ used the word, a few hours after, in a sense that had nothing whatever to do with time. J. xvii. 3 (see Dr. Plumptre in Bp. Ellicott's *Commentary, ad loc.*).

ignorance can dispute,—it cannot be right to read that meaning into the word, because of any *a priori* bias, in other passages. All scholars alike admit that in many places αἰών can only mean "age" and αἰώνιος only age-long, or (in the classic sense of the word) secular, which is often equivalent to "indefinite."[1] Many scholars who have a good right to be heard deny that it ever necessarily means "endless," though it is predicted of endless things. It therefore becomes a clear duty to keep the rendering "eternal," which is a neutral word, and does not mislead the ignorant into supposing that a doctrine has been revealed, which, if revealed at all—which we show good grounds for denying—is most certainly not revealed by the use of that single disputed adjective, or any of its cognate expressions.[2]

---

[1] I have further examined these words in a subsequent Excursus. עֹלָם and עוֹלָם seem to be much more used for an *indefinite* than for an *infinite* time."—Parkhurst. Prof. Bartlett, arguing for the so-called "orthodox" view, uses more than once the phrase "infinite, *or at least indefinite*"—but what very different words! Seventy times out of ninety the word *cannot* mean endless.

[2] All this and my Excursus on the word were written before

I will only add that ἀσβεστὸν πῦρ, "unquenchable fire,"—an expression which no one dreams of taking with slavish literalness when found in other connections,—is mistranslated "fire which *never shall be* quenched;" and that even if this translation were tenable it would not necessarily imply that all who suffer from it should remain for ever in it. But how untenable the translation is cannot be more

Mr. Clemance sent me his little book on *Future Punishment*, and he exactly expresses the facts when he says that αἰών and αἰώνιος are "words which shine only by a reflected light," *i e.* that their meaning depends entirely on the words with which they are joined, so that it is quite false to say that αἰώνιος joined with ζωή must mean the same as αἰώνιος joined with κόλασις. The word means endless in neither clause (see Excursus, p. 199), but, *just as in Rom.* xvi. 25, 26, there is no reason why it *might* not mean *endless* in one, yet have no such meaning in the other. "If good ever should come to an end, that would come to an end which Christ died to bring in ; but if evil comes to an end that comes to an end which He died to destroy. So that the two stand by no means on the same footing," p. 65. "An *æon* may have an end. Æons of æons may have an end. Only that which lasts though *all* the æons is without an end ; and Scripture affirms this only of the kingdom of God, and of the glory of God in the Church. The absolute eternity of evil is nowhere affirmed," p. 86. Very much indeed the reverse is affirmed in the many passages which speak of the Final Restitution.

simply and decisively proved than by the fact that in these passages our Lord is quoting, and in a milder form, the oriental and poetic hyperbole of Isaiah,[1] who, though he uses a stronger form of expression, is speaking of a purely earthly and entirely transient flame.

And, I would ask, if the literal meaning of one or two passages in our Lord's parables is to be pressed to conclusions which even the literal meaning or figurative expressions will not bear, why is no account to be made of the fact that even the unmerciful debtor is only handed over to the tormentors *until* the debt shall have been paid? I will only add—for in the brief space and time at my disposal it is impossible for me to enter exhaustively into the discussion, though otherwise I would gladly show text by text that there is no real Scriptural authority for the popular view, and a vast mass of Scriptural evidence against it—that there are three passages of our Lord's teaching which, though they may be perhaps urged against Universalism, tell most strongly in favour of the views

[1] Is. lxvi. 24.

here maintained. One of these is the judgment pro-
nounced on Judas (Matt. xxvi. 24), "It had been good
(καλόν) for that man if he had not been born ;" another
is the warning to fear him who can destroy both soul
and body in Gehenna (Matt. x. 28) ; a third is the sin
which (according to our version) "shall not be forgiven
either in this world or that which is to come." (Matt.
xii. 32).

1. Now it seems to me that these passages strongly
support the ancient against the common view. Judas
committed the most awful of human crimes : whatever
happened to him hereafter it might well be said it
would have been good (καλόν is untranslatable) for him
if he had never been born.[1] Yet how infinitely milder
is this form of speech than any which we could have
expected, had the common view be true! How absolutely silent is it about torments or their endlessness!

---

[1] Plato speaks in the voice of simple human reason when he
describes some sins as ἰασιμά, and speaks of some men as (humanly)
ἀνίατοι (Gorg. p. 525). Yet Olympiodorus, commenting on the
passage, strikingly observes that, though they have lost the αὐτο-
κίνητον, still ὡς ἑτεροκίνητοι σώζονται (see Prof. Mayor, Contemp.
Rev., May, 1876.)

How strongly does it suggest the conclusion that, for all *except* those who have been guilty of the most enormous crimes, even " æonian punishment " may be more blessed than never to have been ! How utterly do they dis countenance the common view that it would have been better for *most* of our race to have been unborn ! It is most erroneously supposed that those who believe in the possible restoration of many of the lost imply that they will ultimately be admitted into perfect bliss. They hold no such view. The *poena damni*—the loss and partial loss of all that " might have been "—may continue long after the *poena sensûs* has ended. A man's sin may be ultimately forgiven him; he may even attain to a certain degree of peace ; and yet, while the memory of his sin remains, he may be the first to acquiesce in the sorrowful decision that it had been well for him if he had not been born. A cessation of agonising remorse is not the same thing as perfect peace, nor are the alleviations of deserved punishment identical with the beatific vision. All the trite rhetoric which from Tertullian downwards has talked of the impossibility of supposing that ultimately there will be no difference between a John and a Judas, a Jezebel and a Virgin Mary, may be dismissed as entirely futile and beside the mark.

2. The second passage merely attributes to God a power which we know the Omnipotent must possess. He can destroy the soul, but it says not that He will. If any think that this is implied, it seems to me that no logical choice is open to them but to embrace the theory of Conditional Immortality.

3. The third passage has only a disputed bearing on the subject at all. If αἰών be rightly rendered, as in nearly every passage where it occurs it *may* be rightly rendered by "age," our Lord only says that there is one particular sin—and what sin this is, no one has ever known—which is so heinous as not to be pardonable either in this (the Jewish) or the coming (the Christian) dispensation. Nothing therefore is of necessity implied respecting the world beyond the grave. But if it be, how overwhelming is the argument with which I am supplied! *Every sin and blasphemy shall be forgiven,* our Lord says,—without further limitation and with no shadow of a hint that He refers to this life only—a gloss

which indeed His words directly exclude; every sin and blasphemy shall be forgiven here or hereafter—except one! "If one sin only is excluded from forgiveness in that coming age, other sins cannot stand on the same level, and the dimness behind the veil is lit up with at least a gleam of hope."

Further than this, consider how large a sanction is added to all that I have urged by our Lord's saying that some will be punished with few and some with many stripes. Is any conceivable explanation of those words consistent with various degrees of *endlessness* in torture? Consider lastly the whole tenor of His life and teaching, and the statement that, even after death, He "went and preached to the spirits in prison." To the word and to the testimony : if they speak not according to the whole revelation of God's nature and His dealings with man, are we to follow the whole tenor of the revelation, or a few isolated and disputable texts?

And here let those who think that the voice of Scripture is decisive for "endless torments,"—simply because they confuse the voice of Scripture with the necessarily imperfect interpretations of many passages

of it which from age to age are being gradually removed,
—let them meditate on this fact. Their view, if they will
searchingly examine the grounds of it, depends mainly on
two or three scattered texts in the Synoptic Gospels;
texts chiefly aimed, not at the ordinary sinners of
the world, but at Pharisees and their disciples; texts
of which in several instances the true reading is highly
dubious; texts of which the English translation has been
proved to be erroneous; texts of which the current exegesis
is in the highest degree uncertain; texts which learned
and competent critics understand on critical and his-
torical grounds in a sense almost opposite to that in
which they are usually taken; texts so little decisive
that the Church has never built any dogma upon them;
texts which did not prevent the most eloquent, the most
learned, and the most orthodox of Fathers from holding
a view which is falsely asserted to contradict them; texts
which depend for their supposed meaning on a rigid
literalism, the possibility of which is utterly overthrown by
the circumstance that they are absolutely contradicted by
other texts far more numerous, if these latter be interpreted on the same principles; texts of which the

other clause is, in almost every instance, confessedly metaphorical; texts finally, which, if thus understood, rob the Gospel of its most precious elements and run counter to the repeated expressions of Scripture respecting Christ's plenteous redemption and God's fatherly tenderness and everlasting mercy ; — texts therefore which we could not but *hesitate* to interpret in accordance with the popular view, even if we had not the plainest proofs that—even if these passages were *not* limited by others—the popular view of them is historically and logically inadmissible.

Now turn from the first three Gospels to the fourth, and what do we find ? Passages not a few which bear on the Gospel of Hope : not one—so far as I can see —which gives any sanction whatever to the notion of endless torments.

Now turn to the Epistles of the three greatest Apostles. Do we find the popular doctrine in them ? We find multitudes of passages—especially in St. Paul's later epistles —which speak without limit of a final restoration ; but " that the doctrinal writings of these three chief teachers of the Gospel are wholly destitute of any assertions of the endless misery of sinners in the literal sense of the word, can be verified by every reader."[1] Had the doctrine been true, would it have been left to a very few expressions, opposed in their literal meaning to so many others, and in themselves so metaphorical, so shadowy, so uncertain, so more than disputable?

Turning now from the subject of revealed to natural religion, those who uphold the possibility, for many at any rate, of a gradual amelioration beyond the grave, are constantly confronted with the name, the authority, the arguments of Bishop Butler, and with those passages especially in which he warns us that we must not construct after our own fashion an ideal universe, or judge of the arm of God by the finger of man. I have known the writings of Butler for many years, and I entirely accept the cogency of his reasoning. Against the doctrine of those, if such there be, who deny the

---

.[1] Rev. E. White, *Life in Christ*, p. 348. "The Bible," says this devout and deeply reverent writer, "has fallen much into the hands of those who imagine that a few favourite 'texts' will suffice to prove that Omniscience is on the side of even the most extravagant theologies." (See Excursus I. p. 185.)

existence of punishment beyond the grave,—possibly even against Universalism as an *a priori* doctrine— they are irresistible. But beyond this they do not and cannot go. Into the question of "endless torments" Butler does not enter at all; nor does he use one single argument which in any way tells (for instance), against the doctrine of Purgatory.[1] Further than this, I may mention the curious fact that it was a sentence in Bishop Butler's *Analogy* which first set me seriously thinking on this question while I was still a boy, and which seemed to me to have an unanswerable weight in favour of the view which is here advocated. That sentence is as follows:—"Our whole nature leads us to ascribe moral perfection to God, and to deny all imperfection of Him. And this will for ever be a practical proof of His moral character, to such as will

---

[1] "All which can be positively asserted to be matter of mere revelation with regard to this doctrine, seems to be that the great distinction between the righteous and the wicked shall be made at the end of this world ; that each shall then receive according to his deserts." *Analogy*, i. 2, *note*. There is not a word about end-lessness here. "As regards duration," says Mr. Clemance, "revela-tion is relative not absolute." (See Excursus I. p. 185.)

consider what a practical proof is; because it is the voice of God speaking in us. And from hence we conclude that virtue must be the happiness, and vice the misery of every creature; and that regularity, and order, and right cannot but prevail finally in a universe under His government." Opposite to the word " finally" I see written in my edition, the words " and invariably?" and although I was well aware that Bishop Butler might have explained the final prevalence of right in a manner different from the general cessation of evil, yet it was the consideration involved in the only complete acceptance of the words which he there actually uses, which ultimately deepened in my mind the impression which I drew from conscience, from reason, and from God's Holy Word.

What remains to say is merely personal. Knowing how wide is the range, and how infinite the importance of those beliefs respecting which all Christians are agreed, I have always desired to avoid controversy. It is with no fondness for controversy that I publish these sermons, or that I originally preached them. Wishing, in such humble manner as I could, to make the sermons at the Abbey bear on those thoughts, which, since they are so prominent in literature, must also be prominent in the minds of many of those miscellaneous hundreds who there compose our ordinary congregations, I first preached on the subject of Heaven, because the Christian conception of Heaven had been so roughly, and as I thought, mistakenly assailed. Between that day and the next on which it became my turn to preach, circumstances had strongly turned my thoughts towards the future life, and my attention was naturally attracted by the question discussed in one of our reviews, "Is life worth living?" Having answered that question in what seemed to me to be the Christian sense, I was of course immediately faced by the question, "How can life be regarded as worth living by the majority of mankind, if, as is taught by the current religious teaching, they are doomed to everlasting damnation?"

Now as to the common opinions respecting "Hell," it was impossible to be mistaken, and I had myself been trained in them. In these days, indeed, they are seldom stated in all their breadth and all their

horror. Most religious teachers profess to hold them,
but content themselves with a few vague and stray
allusions ; and if pressed on the subject manage in a
thousand ways to get rid of them. They envelop them
in a cloud of modifications and exceptions, and thus
evacuate them of all real significance ; or they so indefinitely extend the conception of repentance, and admit
the validity of a repentance so purely hasty and superficial, as to leave their doctrine in the condition of a
mere dangerous formula without any real bearing on
the ordinary lives of men.   There are hundreds of
volumes of modern sermons by clergymen of all schools
in which you either do not find the word " Hell " at
all, or only in the form of some dim, verbal, and half
apologetic phrase.   Now this common doctrine should
either be held or not held.   If it be indeed a tenet of
our faith, it is one so appalling that it cannot be ob-
truded too incessantly, or too vividly pourtrayed.   But
if, as I believe, the *current opinions* about Hell are *not*
tenets of our faith, they cannot be too honestly or too
distinctly repudiated.

Clergymen of all denominations bewail their utter

inability to prevent the spread of materialism and infidelity. I, for my part, cannot be surprised at this when I feel within me the revolt of an indignant conscience against much which is taught as an essential part of a Gospel of salvation. It was the doctrine of endless torments which made an infidel of the elder Mill.[1] Does the reader suppose that in this respect he stood alone? Those who work among our London artisans know well the effect that the doctrine has on them. Never was there a wilder and more monstrous delusion than that it is efficacious in deterring them from sin ! " I am but thirty-two : I am a coke-burner, which has injured my lungs. I have worked seven days and seven nights, on and off. You see I havn't had my chance," said a poor man to Mrs. Marie Hilton. " Do you really think, master, that God Almighty will put me in fire for ever and ever, after putting me in this here mud all my lifetime ?" asked a rough navvy

---

[1] Mill's *Autobiography*, p. 41. *Three Essays*, p. 114. "Compared with this, every other objection to Christianity sinks into insignificance." It was this, too, that chiefly made Theodore Parker a Unitarian. See p. 204.

d

of a city missionary not long ago.[1] People who sit in their armchairs may show that his theology was very wicked ; but are such minds likely to be restrained by preaching endless torments ? That has been done very amply in all ages ; with what effect ? Sixteen centuries intervened between the time when the first and second of the following passages were penned :—

"Quæ tunc spectaculi latitudo ! quid admirer ? quid rideam ? ubi gaudeam, ubi exsultem, spectans tot et tantos reges . . . . in imis tenebris congemiscentes ? item præsides, persecutores dominici nominis sævioribus flammis quam ipsi sævierunt insultantibus contra Christianos, liquescentes ? præterea sapientes illos philosophos coram discipulis suis una conflagrantibus erubescentes . . . ? etiam poetas non ad Rhadamanthi nec ad Minois, sed ad inopinati Christi tribunal palpitantes ? . . . tunc histriones cognoscendi solutiores multo per ignem ; tunc spectandus auriga in flammeâ rotâ totus rubens ; tunc xystici non in gymnasiis sed in igne jaculati."—*De Spectac.* 30.

So wrote Tertullian centuries ago, and I quote the

[1] White, *Life in Christ*, p. 490 (third ed.).

passage not for its hard savagery—though there certainly are natures in which such savagery is heightened by this belief—but for its ghastly ingenuity. It was in a far more pitying and Christian spirit, but with equal vividness in the imagination of the horrible, that Mr. Spurgeon has written thus :—

"Thou wilt look up there on the throne of God and it shall be written, 'For ever!' When the damned jingle the burning irons of their torment they shall say, 'For ever!' When they howl, echo cries, 'For ever.'"

> "'For ever' is written on their racks,
> 'For ever' on their chains ;
> 'For ever' burneth in the fire,
> 'For ever,' ever reigns."

Can those who dwell on such ghastly imaginations try to realise the significance of these expressions? Such oratory has been heard for many centuries; and although those who have used it may often have done a very blessed work by virtue of their *other* doctrines, there is overwhelming evidence to show that the outcome of such delineations taken alone—were they not rejected as they are by the

instinctive faith of man — could only be hysteria,
terror, and religious madness in the weak; indignant
infidelity or incredulous abhorrence in the strong.
"From the fear of hell," says the Rev. Robert
Suffield, after twenty years' experience as confessor to
thousands while working as "Apostolic Missionary" in
most of the large towns of England, in many por-
tions of Ireland, in part of Scotland, and also in
France—" we never expected virtue or high motives or
a noble life; but we practically found it useless as
a deterrent.   It always influenced the wrong people
and in a wrong way.   It caused infidelity to some,
temptation to others, and misery without virtue to
most. It appealed to the lowest motives and the lowest
characters; not however to deter from vice, but to
make them the willing subjects of sad and often
puerile superstitions." [1]

But if we believe—not the doctrine of future retribution, but—the popular teaching about Hell, with all its
parasitic accretions, to be utterly false—to be an utterly
untenable forcing of the metaphoric language of

[1] Rev. E. White's *Life in Christ*, p. viii. (third ed.).

a misinterpreted parable into frightful literalism and intolerable doctrine—can it be wondered if I strive to set it aside with an energy which has been called violence? I have seen a pamphlet of extracts from Pinamonti and Father Furniss (*permissu superiorum*) containing passages so unutterably revolting, illustrated by woodcuts of such abhorrent atrocity, that even to look at them seemed to involve guilt which called for the performance of a lustration. In reading such passages—involving as they do our entire conception of the character of our Father in Heaven—must not the heart burn with a natural and surely excusable indignation, not against the speakers, but against the things they have said?

For, I would ask the reader kindly to bear in mind that the following sermons were not *conciones ad clerum*, or elaborate theological essays, but as it were sparks from the anvil of a busy life. Under different circumstances I might have given more measured and elaborate utterance to the same convictions; but the necessarily frequent sermons of one who is not blessed with quiet, or leisure, or time to study, can never

resemble the rarer sermons of those to whom it is
"given to contemplate the bright countenance of truth
in the mild and dewy air of delightful studies." They
can only be written roughly and hastily, *currente calamo*,
amid occupations, interruptions, and anxieties of every
kind.[1] Precisely the same doctrines have been preached,
even during the few past months, by learned and
most honoured divines who have, from whatever cause,
escaped the antagonism which I have encountered. But
I shall not for one moment regret that opposition if I
may once more turn the serious thoughts of earnest
and holy men to truths which have been displaced by
groundless opinions, and which are necessary for the
purity, almost for the very existence, of that faith which
is the one sole hope of the suffering world, but which

---

[1] I may perhaps be allowed to mention one single fact. From
the day on which I came to London in September, 1876, till the
day on which I left it for a brief summer holiday, I was not able
to add one word or line to a work on which I have long been
engaged. I mention this not on any personal grounds, but because
I would humbly suggest that the original meaning and object of
canonries is destroyed when they are tied by Act of Parliament
to London livings.

in many thousands of hearts and minds has been utterly shipwrecked upon the reef of this merely human opinion about "endless torments for the vast majority, as a doom passed irreversibly at death."

And now, in all humility, I submit to the judgment of all wise and good men in the Church of God the views which I have thus suddenly been called upon to advocate. I sincerely ask pardon if any of my expressions cause an unintended irritation ;—I beg a kindly consideration for any error which may be due to the haste in which I have been forced to prepare this volume ;—I pray God that whether by the confirmation, or by the refutation, of what I have urged, this truth may be elicited ;—I assure all good people who may be unable to accept these views that they are due at the worst to an *error in intellectu,* not to any *contumacia in voluntate ;*—and I feel assured of this at any rate, that no true Christian—even if he be unable to adopt my conclusions—will cherish any anger or hatred against a doctrine which alone can stem the spread of infidelity; which is maintained in a spirit of perfect loyalty to the Church, and of reverence for her most holy faith ;

which is supported on strong Scriptural authority;
which is sincerely believed to be a truer explanation
of the words of our Lord and Master than that by
which it has too often been superseded; and which
seems to those who hold it to be impregnably built
upon the rock of an entire belief in Christ's infinite
Redemption and of the mercy "from everlasting to
everlasting" of Him whose name is Love.

> " Behold, we know not anything ;
>   I can but trust that good shall fall
>   At last—far off—at last, to all,
>   And every winter change to spring.
>
> " So runs my dream : but what am I ?
>   An infant crying in the night :
>   An infant crying for the light :
>   And with no language but a cry."

CHRISTMAS EVE, 1877.   .

CONTENTS.

ETERNAL HOPE.

"The wish, that of the living whole
  No life may fail beyond the grave,
  Derives it not from what we have
The likest God within the soul?"

TENNYSON, *In Memoriam.*

SERMONS.

SERMON I.

WHAT HEAVEN IS.[1]

HEB. iv. 11.

"Let us labour therefore to enter into that rest."

IN one of our ablest Reviews,[2] a discussion has been going on for some time on the soul and future life; and it is a sign of the large toleration of the times that some of the writers not only glory in expressing a belief that, apart from his body, man has no soul, and no life beyond the grave—an opinion, the open expression of which would, twenty years ago have been received with

---

[1] Preached in Westminster Abbey, Oct. 14, 1877.
[2] *The Nineteenth Century.*

S   B

outbursts of indignation; but have even arrived at the point of treating with compassionate disdain those who still cling to the traditional belief. Now I do not think it needful, brethren, in this nine-teenth century after Christ, to argue with you that you have souls, and that your life is not as the life of the beasts that perish. To the end of time the human race will believe this, though from the dawn of History there have been a few philosophers who disputed it. *Securus judicat orbis terrarum.* These speculations have never shaken, will never shake, the fixed convictions of mankind. Those convictions might have been expressed from very early ages in the simple verse of the poet—

> " Life is real, life is earnest,
>   And the grave is not its goal ;
>   'Dust thou art, to dust returnest,'
>   Was not spoken of the soul."

We may freely concede that, of the separate existence of the immaterial soul, and our survival beyond "the intolerable indignities of dust to dust," we have no mathematical demonstration to offer. But this fact does not in the slightest degree trouble us, because neither is there any such proof of the existence of a God. It is perfectly easy for a man to say, if he will, ' I do not believe in a God.' I do not care to offer up any worship, even of the silent sort, even at the altar of "the unknown and the unknowable." I do not even think it worth while to pray that wild prayer once uttered by a criminal upon the scaffold, " O God, if there be a God, save my soul, if I have a soul." A man may say all this, and plume himself on this melancholy abnegation of man's fairest hopes ; on this deliberate suicide of the spiritual faculty ; and if he considers such opinions to be a sign of intellectual emancipation, we can offer to him no proof that will necessarily convince him. When Vanini [1] lay in prison on a charge of atheism, he touched with his foot

---

[1] The story is also told of Galileo.

a straw which lay on his dungeon-floor, and said, "that from that straw he could prove the existence of God." We can pluck the meanest flower of the hedgerow, and point to the exquisite perfection of its structure, the tender delicacy of its loveliness; we may pick up the tiniest shell out of myriads upon the shore, so delicate that a touch would crush it, and yet a miracle of rose and pearl, of lustrous iridescence and fairy arabesque, and ask the atheist if he feels seriously certain that these things are but the accidental outcome of self-evolving laws. We can take him under the canopy of night, and show him the stars of heaven, and ask him whether he really holds them to be nothing more than "shining illusions of the night, eternal images of deception in an imaginary heaven, golden lies in dark-blue nothingness."[1] Or we may bid him watch with us the flow of the vast stream of history, and see how the great laws of it are as mighty currents

[1] Heine, *Confessions* (Stigand's *Life of Heine*, i. 50).

"that make for righteousness." Or we may appeal
to the inner voices of his being, and ask whether
they have indeed no message to tell him. But if
he deny or reject such arguments as these; if he
treat with arrogant scorn that evidence of the
things unseen which has been enough in all ages
for the millions of humanity—which was enough
in past times for Dante and Shakespeare, and
Milton, and Newton—which was enough till yesterday for Brewster, and Whewell, and Herschel, and
Faraday :—if he demand a kind of proof which is
impossible, and which God has withheld, seeing that
it is a law that spiritual things can only be spiritually discerned, and that we walk by faith and
not by sight,—if, in short, a man will not see
God because clouds and darkness are round about
Him, although righteousness and judgment are the
habitation of His seat : then we can do no more.
He must believe or not believe—he must bear or
must forbear, as seems him best. We cannot
argue about colour to the blind. We cannot prove

the glory of music to the deaf. If a man shuts his eyes hard, we cannot make him see the sun. "That the blush of morning is fair, that the quietude of grief is sacred, that the heroism of conscience is noble, who will undertake to *prove* to one who does not see it ? So wisdom, beauty, holiness, are immeasurable things, appreciable by pure perception, but which no rule can gauge, no argument demonstrate."[1] My brethren, if you know God, or rather are known of Him, you will need no proof that He is, and that He is the rewarder of them that diligently seek Him ; and you will not be much troubled by the scepticism of philosophers. Oh, let us get near to God by faith and prayer, and we shall break with one of our fingers through the brain-spun meshes of these impotent negations. Prove to us that by the word "God" we ought only to mean "vortices of atoms," or "streams of tendency," and at the end of such triumphant demonstrations, we shall but kneel

[1] Martineau, *Hours of Thought.*

down before Him who made us, and not we ourselves, and with bowed head, and sad yet kindling
heart, shall pray, if possible, with yet deeper conviction, " Our Father which art in Heaven." And
when we thus believe in Him whom we have not
seen, all else follows. We believe that He did not
befool with irresistible longings, that He did not
deceive with imaginary hopes, the man whom
He had made. We believe that the breath of life
which came from Him shall not pass away. We
believe that He sent His Son to die for us and to
save us. We believe that because He lives we
shall live also. We believe; we are content; we
do not even ask for further proof. In this belief,
which we believe that He inspireth, we shall con-
sole ourselves amid all the emptiness and sorrow
of life; we shall advance, calm and happy, to the
very grave and gate of death.

2. I speak to Christians; to Christians who
hope not only to live, but to live in heaven
hereafter; and I want this morning to fix your

contemplation upon that heaven, and to ask
what are our thoughts of it, and why. And I do
this partly because one of the ablest and most
eloquent of the writers to whom I have alluded
has spoken with passionate scorn of what he
supposes to be our anticipations of heaven, and
of what he is pleased to represent as the necessary
result of such anticipations. He says that we
are looking for a "vacuous eternity;" "a future
of ceaseless psalmody," "an eternity of the
tabor," "so gross, so sensual, so indolent, so
selfish," that the belief in it "paralyses practical
life, and throws it into discord." "A life of
vanity in a vale of tears, followed by an infinity
of celestial rapture," is, he says, "necessarily a
life of infinitesimal importance," making men
"dull to the moral responsibility which, in its
awfulness, begins only at the grave," and "little
influenced by the futurity which will judge
them." "And why," he asks, "should this great
end, staring at all of us along the vista of each

human life, be for ever a matter of dithyrambic hypotheses and evasive tropes?"[1]

Now I shall offer you no "dithyrambic hypotheses," or "evasive tropes," but, eloquent as all this is, I am sure that the most thoughtful of you must have listened to it with amused bewilderment. It must have been just a little incongruous and unreal to you to hear the Christian's hope of heaven described as though it were some Mohammedan paradise,—as being not only gross, selfish, and sensual, but also as paralysing and immoral,—when you know what lives it has influenced, what deeds it has inspired. Were the hopes of St. Stephen, think you, dull and immoral, when, with face radiant as the face of an angel, he gazed into the opening heavens? Was it a dull selfishness which inspired the martyrs as they bathed their hands in the torturing flame, or which nerved the Christian maiden as she knelt awaiting with a smile the

[1] Mr. Frederic Harrison, *Nineteenth Century*, i. 834, &c.

tiger's spring? Was it a paralysing superstition which fills with "tempestuous glory" the sufferings of the good; which breathed through the calm last words of Richard Hooker; which made Addison tell the young Earl of Warwick to see how a Christian could die; which inspired the eager "Lord, open to me, open to me," of the dying Lacordaire; or which has enabled so many thousands of Christians, in every age and every country, to become lovelier in spirit during each hour of life's waning lustre, showing ever "a sublimer faith, a brighter hope, a kinder sympathy, a gentler resignation?" Ah no! my brethren, "the rattling tongue of saucy and audacious eloquence" will never persuade you of this; and you will only listen with a smile when you are assured that the hopes which uplifted such lives, and glorified such ends, were but the confusing fumes of a puerile illusion. We *know* not indeed ;—but we *believe.* We walk by faith, though we cannot walk by sight. But were the arguments of these philosophers ten thousand times more cogent than they are,

> " What can we do, o'er whom the unbeholden
>   Hangs in a night wherewith we dare not cope ?
> What but look sunward, and with faces golden
>   Speak to each other softly of hope ? "

It will take many a ream of agonistic and nihilistic literature to rob us of the conviction with which we say, " I believe in God the Father, and God the Son, and God the Holy Ghost; I believe in the Communion of Saints, in the forgiveness of sins, the Resurrection of the body, and the Life Everlasting. Amen."

3. Well then, my brethren, we believe in Heaven : but what is Heaven ? Our friends die—men die by myriads ; at every ticking of the clock some fifty souls have passed away ;—yet not a breath of sound shakes the curtain of impenetrable darkness which hangs between us and the unseen world. A fair child sighs away his innocent soul, and in a moment, perhaps,

> " He hath learnt the secret hid
> Under either pyramid ;—"

but to his parents, in their agony, comes no faintest whisper from the intervital gloom. Not to one of all the unnumbered generations whose dust is blown upon the desert winds has it been permitted to breathe one syllable or letter of the dim and awful secret beyond the grave. And yet the faith of man has not been shaken, nor, for all this deep, unbroken silence, has he ever ceased to believe that He who called us into being will bless, will save, will cherish the souls which He hath made. We feel sure He did not mean us merely "to be born weeping, to live complaining, and to die disappointed," and so cease to be, but that He has a new home for us in other worlds. It is the *fact* which we believe ; the details are not revealed to us. And hence each race has fancied its own ideal of heaven.

> "Lo ! the poor Indian, whose untutored mind
> Sees God in clouds, or hears Him in the wind,

His soul proud science never taught to stray
Far as the solar walk and milky way,
Yet simple nature to his hope has given
Behind the cloud-capt hills a humbler heaven.

 *   *   *   *

To be content 's his natural desire,
He asks no angel's wing, no seraph's fire,
But thinks, admitted to that equal sky,
His faithful dog shall bear him company."

The Greek had his Elysian plains, where the Eidôla — the shadowy images of the dead — moved in a world of shadows; and his Islands of the Blest, where Achilles and Tydides unlaced the helmets from their flowing hair.[1] The Scandinavian dreamed of his green Paradise hereafter amid the waste. Few indeed have been the nations who have not imagined that there remains for holy souls beyond the grave some

"Island valley of Avilion,
Where falls not hail or rain, or any snow,
Nor ever wind blows loudly."

---

[1] νεκύων ἀμενηνὰ κάρηνα, *Od.* x. 521 ; iv. 503. εἴδωλα καμόντον, *Od.* xi. 476. μακάρων νῆσοι, Hes. Op. 169 ; Pind. *Ol.* ii. 129.

And all Christians, that they may be enabled to
give some form to that which cannot be uttered,[1]
have dwelt with rapture on the glowing symbols
of the poet of the Apocalypse—the New Jerusalem descending out of heaven from God, having
the glory of God, and her light like unto a stone
most precious, even unto a jasper stone; and the
gates of pearl, and the foundations of precious
stones, and the pure river of the water of life,
clear as crystal, and the Tree of Life, with its
leaves for the healing of the nations.[2]   Symbols
only,—yet exquisite symbols of the poet's vision,
which dull philosophies may scorn, but in which
a Dante and a Milton delighted ; symbols which
come back to us with the freshness and the sweet-
ness of childhood, as we sing the hymns, so dear
to Christian worship, of " Jerusalem the golden,"
or " There is a land of pure delight."   Yet even
these symbolic passages do not thrill the heart

---

[1] 2 Cor. xii. 4, 5, ἄῤῥητα ῥήματα.
[2] Rev. xxi. xxii. xiv.

so keenly as others, which speak with scarce a symbol, and simply tell of a life without life's agonies, and the vision of God undarkened by mists of sin. " They shall hunger no more, neither thirst any more; neither shall the sun light on them, nor any heat. For the Lamb that is in the midst of the throne shall feed them, and shall lead them unto living fountains of waters ; and God shall wipe away all tears from their eyes."[1] "And there shall be no more curse, but the throne of God and of the Lamb shall be in it ; and His servants shall serve Him ; and they shall see His face, and His name shall be in their foreheads."[2] And if we need *any* symbols to help us, they are symbols of transparent meaning ; green meadows, where men may breathe God's fresh air, and see His golden light ; glorified cities, with none of the filth and repulsiveness of these, but where no foul step intrudes ; white robes, pure emblem of stain- less innocence ; the crown, and the palm-branch,

[1] Rev. vii. 16, 17.   [2] Rev. xxii. 3, 4.

and the throne of serene self-mastery over our spiritual enemies ; and the golden harp, and the endless song,—which do but speak of abounding happiness, in that form of it which is, of all others, the most innocent, the most thrilling, the most intense.

4. To say that there is anything "dull, gross, selfish, sensual" here, is surely an abuse of words. But if you cannot rest in these emblems, there is *yet* a more excellent way. If you still sigh,—

> " O for a nearer insight into heaven,
> More knowledge of the glory and the joy
> Which there unto the happy souls is given,
> Their intercourse, their worship, their employ ;
> For it is past belief that Christ hath died
> Only that we unending psalms may sing ;
> That all the gain Death's awful curtains hide
> In this eternity of antheming—" [1]

—if you say this, do not fear ;—there are other conceptions of heaven which do not deal in imagery at all. What may be the physical conditions of

[1] Poems by T. Lynch.

Heaven we cannot tell, and perhaps the very phrase may be meaningless of that place where they neither marry nor are given in marriage, but are as the angels of God.[1] But so far as Heaven is a place at all, its fundamental conception is that it is a place where sin is not. "Without are dogs."[2] No guilty step may pass the gates of pearl, no polluting presence fling shadows on the golden streets. They who live there are the angels, and just men made perfect, and the spirits of the saints in light. And if we ever get there, we shall be as they; for to be there is to see the face of God, and to see the face of God is to be changed into the same image from glory to glory.[3] There life's stains shall have been purged away ; and the gold shall be mixed with dross no longer ; nor the fine gold dim. There is no slander there ; no envy, no hatred ; no malice ; no lies. There is no murder there, nor wounds, nor war. The filth of drunkenness is not in that city of God. No

---

[1] Matt. xxii. 30.   [2] Rev. xxii. 15.   [3] 2 Cor. iii 18.

C

bleared and blighted crowds, degraded out of the semblance of humanity, crawl like singed moths, round the flaring houses of multiplied temptations. There are no hearts depraved, corrupted, eaten out by lust; no victims of man's brutal selfishness, no witnesses of his utter shame. Ah, my brethren, which of us all looking back does not sigh, 'I am not all that I might have been ; I might have been noble, and I have not been noble ; I might have been kind, and I have not been kind ; I might have been pure, and I have not been pure'? Would you not think it almost a Heaven if, without giving you anything fresh at all, God would but give you back what once He gave ? If He would but restore to you the sweet innocent childhood He once bestowed, that having learnt now that sin is anguish, and that good is best, you might not ravage the fair vineyard of your life, or lay waste its inner sanctities ? Ah no ! perhaps not, for you feel that you might only fall again ; only be a prodigal again ; only be weak and base and vile again, only despair again of what you feel to be sweetest, and barter for the degraded present the future immortality. But oh, to have been disenchanted utterly, for ever, from the low aims of the world! oh, to have been set free for ever from the yoke of habit and the power of temptation! oh, to desire only, and to do only what is good, without evil being ever present to us! oh, to do perfectly, what here we have but imperfectly attempted! oh, to *be*, what here we have only seemed to be or wished to be! oh, to be honest, true, noble, sincere, genuine, pure, holy to the heart's inmost core! Is not that Heaven? is it dull, gross, sensual, selfish, to sigh for that? Is it not a state rather than a place? is it not a temper rather than a habitation? is it not *to be something* rather than to *go somewhere?* Yes, this, this is Heaven. What more we know not. In other stars, amid His countless worlds, for all we know God may have work for us to do. Who knows what radiant ministrations; what infinite activities; what never-ending progress; what immeasurable happiness;

C 2

what living ecstasies of unimaginable rapture,
where all things are lovely, honourable, pure ; where
there is no moral ugliness; where repulsive squalor,
and degraded art, and insane desire, and loathly
vice, and pinching selfishness, shall be no more ;
where boyhood shall not so live as to make its own
manhood miserable; where manhood shall not so
live as to make old age dishonourable ; where old
age shall not so live as to make death ghastly.
This, this is heaven ! And why should we not
believe that the God who is so good to us hath
such good things in store for all who love Him ?
All the good and true, all the pure and noble, shall
be there :

> " To Milton's trump
> The high groves of the renovated earth
> Unbosom their glad echoes ; inly hushed,
> Adoring Newton, his serener eye
> Raises to heaven."

And all on earth who have ever been high and sweet
and worthy, out of every tribe, and kindred, and
nation, and language,—ten thousand times ten

thousand, and thousands of thousands! Oh, if this be a dull, gross, selfish, sensual conception, give us a greater and better that we may live on it; for we can conceive none lovelier than this, and to us *this* is Heaven.

5. Let us labour, therefore, to enter into that rest: For, my brethren, if, as we Christians believe, Christ hath died to give us entrance into such a Heaven as this, we must believe the same Gospel which tells us, not obscurely, that it is not a reward but a continuity, not a change but a development. To *go there* you must *be thus*. It is shocking to hear men and women talk glibly of "going to Heaven," whose whole lives, and well-nigh every action of their lives,—whose daily words, whose daily deeds, whose very professions,—are disgracing and embittering earth. If we desire Heaven we must seek it here—if we love Heaven we must love it now. And thou—oh, mean, greedy, avaricious, money-loving soul, whose gaze, even in Heaven, would

be on the trodden gold of its pavement;—and thou, base usurer. and defrauder, who, hasting to be rich, carest not how little thou art innocent, and whose path in life is wet with orphans' tears; what hast thou to do with Heaven? there are no cheatings, or swindlings, or hoardings there. And thou, slanderous whisperer, whose soul is venomous with hate and envy; and thou, drunkard, who livest only to drown thy senses in wallowing degradation; and thou, slave of thy lowest lusts, whose uncleanness adds unspeakably to the shames and miseries of earth; and thou, selfish seducer, not afraid

> " To pluck the rose
> From the fair forehead of a maiden shame,
> And set a blister there; "

and thou who hatest thy brother with all but murderous detestation; and thou, bad youth, whose soul is full of fatal ignorance and sensual conceit, and who art drawing iniquity with cords of vanity, and sin as it were with a cart-rope; and all ye, children of wickedness, not slaves only, but willing slaves of Satan, who go as the ox to the slaughter, and as the fool to the correction of the stocks; if *ye* talk of Heaven, what have ye to do with Heaven? Think you that greed, and malice, and intoxication, and debauchery find entrance there? Is there not a lie in your right hands? Think ye to enter Heaven thus in all your vileness, meanness, falsity? Think ye that the apples of Sodom and the clusters of Gomorrah can grow in the same soil with the Tree of Life? Oh, while you know what you are, and are what you are, and yet will not be other than what you are, you would not be happy if God placed you there to-morrow. Every pure look of it would be a burning reproach to you; every rapture of it a burden, every nobleness a shame. If you went there with heart yet unchanged, you would carry hell with you to Heaven, and would make Heaven itself a hell. It could only be Heaven at all by your absence so long as—oh, mark this—so long as you are what now you are. But oh, you can be different; you can be converted; you can repent. Burdens to yourselves, curses to the world, you can yet become true sons of God; you, even you, may enter the gates of pearl, and cast no shadow on the golden streets. For does not God love you, even you? Did not He die for you, even you? Your souls are worthless to all but His infinite love, but *He* in His divine pity, did not think them worthless; for their life He died. Oh! repent ere it be too late, and be what now you are not, and be all that God meant you to be. " Wash you, make you clean, put away the evil of your doings from before God's eyes; cease to do evil; learn to do well." Repent; and *then* look towards Heaven. Put away the love of money, and ask God to give you His true riches. Put away selfishness, and ask God to give you the Spirit of His holy love. Put away lying, and be sincere. Put away conceit, and in the ashes of your self-abasement, tie round you with knots the

sackcloth of humility.[1]   Put away impurity, and
ask God to give you a clean heart and put a
right spirit within you.   Ay, so shall you begin
to know what Heaven is! so shall you begin
to have a foretaste of its happiness, even amid
the sorrows of earth.   So shall there be in your
own hearts, amid all darknesses, a circle of radiant
peace.   Oh, you shall need the aid of no symbols,
for you will think of Heaven not as of some
meadow of asphodel beside the crystal waters, or
golden city in the far-off blue, but as an extension,
as a development, as an undisturbed continuance
of righteousness, and peace, and joy in believing;
you shall know that, whatever else it be or
mean, Heaven means holiness; " Heaven means
principle ; "[2] Heaven means to be one with God.

---

[1] 1 Pet. v. 5.   τὴν ταπεινοφροσύνην ἐγκομβώσασθε (κόμβος, vincu-
lum nodosum).   " Induite, ut amictus humilitatis nullâ vi vobis
detrahi possit."—BENGEL.

[2] This is one of the finest sayings of Confucius.

SERMON II.

IS LIFE WORTH LIVING ?[1]

Ps. lxxix. 14.
"So we that are Thy people, and sheep of Thy pasture, will give
Thee thanks for ever ; and will always be shewing forth Thy
praise, from generation to generation."

As the first day of this month was the grand
festival of All Saints, so in past centuries the second
of November was set apart in honour of " All
Souls." The motives which led to its abolition
were doubtless adequate at the time, but yet we
may be allowed to regret its abandonment. Un-
doubtedly there was a certain grandeur, a certain
catholicity, a certain triumphant faith, a certain

---

[1] Preached at Westminster Abbey, Nov. 4, 1877.

indomitable hope in that ancient commemoration of the departed.[1]   It was the feast of *All* Souls. It is true that it was originally intended only for the faithful departed ; for the souls in purgatory. But in the title of the day at any rate there was no exception made.   On that day men might think, if they would, of all the souls, of all the innocent little ones that have passed away like a breath of vernal air since time began ; of all the souls which the great, and the wise, and the aged, have sighed forth in pain and weariness after long and noble lives ; of all the souls of the wild races of hunters and fishermen in the boundless prairies or the icy floes ; of all the souls that have passed, worn and heavy-laden, from the roaring city-streets ; of all the souls of those whose life has ebbed away in the red tide of unnumbered battles, or whose bodies have been dropped into the troubled waves unknelled, uncoffined, and, save to their God, unknown ; of all

---

[1] It is said to have been founded in the ninth century by Odilon, abbot of Cluny.

the souls even of the guilty, and of the foolish, and of the miserable, and of those who have rushed by wild self-murder into their Maker's presence. All Souls' Day was a day of supplication for, of commemoration of, all these. For these too are souls that He created ; into these too He breathed the breath of life ; and all these lie in the hollow of His hand as the snows of the countless water lilies— whether white and immaculate, or torn and stained —lie all on the silver bosom of the lake. Yes, there is a grandeur and sublimity in the thought of all human souls, as one by one they have passed away and been taken to the mercy of the Merciful ; and a day might well have been set apart to commemorate, in all humble reverence, their awful immortality. Our finite imaginations may grow dizzy at the thought of these infinite multitudes,— these who at each ticking of the clock pass from the one thousand millions of the living ; the tribes, the generations, the centuries, the millenniums, the æons of the dead ; all of which are but the leaves

—green or fallen—of the mighty Tree of Existence ;
—the wave after wave of its illimitable tide. As we
think of all these souls, we recall the imagination
of the great poet of the *Inferno*, and seem to be
gazing on a white, rushing, indistinguishable whirl
of life, sweeping on and on and on, from horizon
to horizon, in ever-lengthening cycles and infinite
processions, endless, multitudinous, innumerable,
as the motes that people the sun's beam.[1]   To us,
inevitably, in this infinitude, all individuality is lost ;
human numeration reels at it.   But it is not so with
Him to whom is known the number of the stars
of heaven, and the sands of the sea, and by whom

> " Every leaf in every nook,
>   Every wave in every brook,"

---

[1] " E dietro la venia si lunga tratta
      Di gente, ch' io non avrei mai creduto
      Che morte tanta n' avesse disfatta."
                              DANTE, *Inferno*, iii. 55.

   "La bufera infernal, che mai non resta,
   Mena gli spirti con la sua rapina."—*Ibid*, v. 31.

are heard as they sing forth their unending
Pæan all day long. And knowing this, we are
not appalled at the thought of these vast multitudes, whose bodies are now the dust of the solid
earth, even though so many millions of them have
passed away in sin and sorrow, because we can say
with the Holy Psalmist of Israel, " O let the sorrowful sighing of the prisoners come before Thee,
according to the greatness of Thy power, save Thou
those that are appointed to die : so we, that are
Thy people and sheep of Thy pasture, shall give
Thee thanks for ever, and shall alway be shewing
forth Thy praise from generation to generation."

2. But if we cannot say this at all, if we
have lost all faith in God, how does life appear
to us then?   There are, alas ! many who have
lost their faith in God.   My brethren, it is not
for us to judge them or to blame them; nay,
we most heartily pity them ; not believe me, with
any supercilious sense of superiority; not with any
Pharisaic taint of pride, but for their own sakes,

and in sincere and humble brotherhood of sympathy, even if they reject or despise such sympathy.
Knowing how terrible, how irreparable, would be
the loss of such faith to *us*, we regret their loss ;
and we pray that they, no less than we, may be
folded at last in the arms of God's infinite mercy,
and led into the radiance of His Eternal Light.
But seeing that the faith of their childhood and of
their fathers has suffered shipwreck ; seeing that
they think, or think that they think, that there is
no God, and that we die as the beasts of the field,
we cannot wonder that they ask themselves
whether life be at all worth the living. Nay, we
are glad that they should discuss such questions ;
because the deeper their bark sinks, the more sure
we are that they must at last reach that bed on
which the ocean rests,—that God, whose offspring
we all are, and in whom, whether we deny Him or
have faith in Him, we all live and move, and have
our being.

3. But since this question is now being deli-

berately discussed, "Is life worth living?" ought we
not, as Christians, to face it, quite fearlessly and
quite faithfully? It is not desirable surely that we
should separate the pulpit from the thoughts of
the week-day world, or avoid the questions which
those who reject and those who scorn religion
discuss among themselves. I do not believe, my
brethren, in the faith which can only be sheltered
by an effeminate clericalism, or a professional con-
ventionality. For myself, I desire that the creed
of a Christian clergyman should be a manly
creed, not afraid to be assaulted—not anxious to
be spoken of with bated breath. I wish that it
should be no mere exotic, which must be kept
under glass lest any wind of heaven should visit
it too roughly; but that it should be rather like
the green blade of the corn, which every rain-
storm may drench, and on which the snow may
lie, and over which the scorching heat may burn
and the chill wind blow, but which, because God's
sunlight falls on it, and it has a principle of life

within, in spite of, nay because of, every freezing
or blighting influence, grows up from the tender
blade to the green ear, and from the green ear
to the rich and ripened corn.

4. Is then life worth living? Life, I mean,
regarded by itself; life on this earth; life apart
from God; your life, my life, human life in
general, considered under its purely earthly aspects
and relationships? Let us glance at this question,—it *must* be inadequately; it may be mistakenly; it may be quite superficially, but yet
(which God grant us!) with the one merit of a
humble endeavour after perfect honesty.

5. And, in answering the question, let us, my
brethren, in no wise exaggerate. Let no personal
circumstances, let no melancholy temperament,
let no pressure of immediate,[1] and it may be
passing, trials bias our verdict. Let us, so far
as may be, look at life steadily and whole. It

---

[1] Frater unicus abiit ad plures.—*Prid. Non. Nov.* Pater optimus.
—*VI. Kal. Jul.* MDCCCLXXVI.

D

is not all darkness; it has its crimson dawns, its rosy sunsets. It is not all clouds; it has its silver embroideries, its radiant glimpses of heaven's blue. It is not all winter; it has its summer days on which "it is a luxury to breathe the breath of life."

> " Life hath its May, and all is joyous then ;
> The woods are vocal, and the winds breathe music,
> The very breeze has mirth in it."

Ask the happy little child with its round checks, and bright eyes, and flaxen curls, and pure sweet face, and the tender, tender love and care that enfold, and encircle, and treasure it, and smooth its path the whole day long; ask the happy boy, tingling with life to the finger-tips, making the fields ring with his glad voice on summer holidays, happy in unselfish friendships, in generous impulses, in strong health, in the freedom from all care, in the confidence of all hopes, when "the boy's will is the wind's will, and the thoughts of youth are long;" ask happy lovers, when they

know the joy of being all in all to each other,
and to their glad gaze

> " A livelier emerald twinkles in the grass,
> A deeper sapphire melts into the sea !"

Ask soldiers in the hour of victory; ask great
thinkers when some immortal truth bursts upon
them ; ask the happy band who gather in the yet
unbroken circle round the Christmas hearth :—or,
take less thrilling moments, and ask fathers and
mothers when cares do not press, and the little ones
are gone to bed, and they sit together by the fireside
through the quiet winter eve : at such times, perhaps, all these will be inclined to tell you that
life *is* worth the living. And though such hours
come not to all, and come not alike to the good
and evil, to the wise and foolish, yet we all do
have peaceful periods of our lives ; quiet intervals
at least between storm and storm ; *interspaces* of
sunlight between the breadths of gloom ; until
over every one of us the night at last sweeps down.

5. Yes, my brethren, let us acknowledge—let us cherish,—let us be grateful for,—let us, as far as we may without selfishness, multiply these natural pleasures, these simple, or innocent, or holy joys. Let us admit, too, that God is very, very good to us, and that the worst evils of our lives are often in anticipation only, and of our own making, not of God's. The Christian is no *pessimist* to encourage in himself a view of life needlessly discouraging; he is no *ascetic*, thinking that God cares for pain or sorrow for pain and sorrow's sake ; he is no *cynic*, who walks of choice in avenues of cypress. And yet if I ask you honestly whether these golden threads of happiness are many enough, or strong enough, to weave either the warp or woof of life, I think I know what your answer must be. Let us grant that childhood at least—keen as are its little trials—is yet rarely otherwise than happy, and that its tears are dried as swiftly as the dew upon the rose. Let us grant, too, that boyhood, though St.

Augustine truly says that the boy's sufferings are as
great while they last as those of a man, is generally
happy; happier since the day when Arnold raised
the whole tone of our public schools, happier since
the day when Shelley abhorred the petty tyrannies
of Eton, and the life of a shrinking, sensitive boy
whose name was William Cowper was darkened
here at Westminster.   And yet not always happy,
I think; and sometimes the source, through life,
of the saddest memories and consequences; and
forgetful, too often, of the "inevitable congruity
between seed and fruit."   But when swiftly, imper-
ceptibly, boyhood and youth are over, and manhood with all its cares is upon us; when the golden
gates close for ever behind us, and we step forth
into the thorny wilderness; when the splendid
vision fades into the light of common day; when
the brilliant ideals and innocent enthusiasms of
early years have been smirched, and vulgarised,
and dimmed; when not one single ray of illusion
or of enchantment rests, were it but for one

instant, over the bleak hills and barren wilderness of life ;—worn men and weary women—ye
who must work, and ye who must weep—how
is it with us then ?

6. My brethren, I will not take any one of the
great *crimes* of life, such as every now and then
they are revealed to us, when the lurid gaze of publicity is cast upon the interior of some suburban
villa or small farm. Clergymen and physicians
know well that these are more common than are
ever made known. I cannot doubt that among these
hundreds gathered here in this Abbey there must
be one or other on whose conscience there lies
the burden of some deadly undiscovered sin. On
all of us sin strives to creep with serpent rustlings,
silent, gradual, stealthy ; or to bound from am-
bush, sudden, irresistible, with tiger springs ;
and there must be some here who have been
stricken with that poison or crushed beneath that
wild beast's force. But I will take no such cases
as that of the clever, handsome youth sinking

step by step into dissipation, into forgery, into shame unspeakable, and the felon's end ; or as that of one who had lived his life honourably before men, tempted by fatal money into crooked ways, and pleading, with tremulous voice, against a sentence which to him has the agony of death. I will not even take the too common case of the man who wakes suddenly to the horrible truth that he is a drunkard, or under the fatal spell of some craving appetite. Who shall say 'I am safe' even from such falls? Yet I will not take these great crimes of life ; nor yet will I take its great *tragedies*. Who has not known cases in which some man has been suddenly beaten down to earth, bruised, bleeding, under the shock of some wholly unexpected, some quite intolerable, catastrophe? Who has not seen families, bright and prosperous, the whole happiness of whose hearth has been shattered, in one moment, as by the crash of doom? Who shall say 'I and mine are safe from these'? Yet I will not take these cases.

No, but I will take the common, common every-day cases of life; life's daily fever; life's necessary trials. My brethren, our sorrows are quite different sorrows; but which of all of us—be he rich or poor, be he noble or insignificant, be he senator or shop-boy,—is exempt from them? Take *pain:* is there one of us who has not known the throbbing head, the aching nerve, the sleepless night? Take *health:* are there none here who rarely know what perfect health is? Take *reputation:* have we not been in anguish when cruel and false things—or in yet deeper anguish when cruel things and true things have been said of us? Take *home:* is there no household whose graves have been scattered far and wide? No father who has seen the dust sprinkled over the golden head of his dear little child? No mother whose heart has not ceased to ache since Death plucked her " wee white rose"? No husband from whom the light of his eyes has been taken at a stroke? No lonely

man, whose circle has ever narrowed and narrowed,
and whose path in life has been marked by the
gravestones of his early friends? And, short of
death, are there no parents whose sons have wrung
their hearts by folly and ingratitude; who have,
in some far land, a prodigal who will come back
no more? And, of all the hundreds who are
listening to the voice of a weak fellow-sinner
like themselves, are there not some—perhaps
many—whose hopes do but seem to dwindle and
dwindle as life goes on; on whom morning never
dawns, but it dawns upon heavy cares, as they
think with a sigh of the dreary routine before
them; of the insufficient means which hamper
them; of the debts that hang like a millstone
about their necks; of the chill discouragement of
helpless and burdened poverty? And are there
not some who look forward, almost with agony
to their day of death, and think how, mayhap,
they must leave their dear ones—loved wife, and
little sons, and little daughters—unprotected and

unprovided for, to the cold pity and grudging
charity of a frosty world? How many might
almost sing with the poet as he sat in deep dejection on the shore,

> " Alas ! I have nor hope, nor health,
>   Nor peace within, nor calm around ;
>   Nor that content, surpassing wealth,
>   The sage in contemplation found ;
>   * ,   *   *   *   *
>   Others there are whom these surround,
>   Smiling they live, and call life pleasure ;
> To me that cup hath been dealt in far other measure."[1]

For, alas, my brethren, I have not yet told anything like the worst ! A man may bear up against
sorrow. He may think it no great matter whether
he be happy or unhappy. If life be not sweet
to him, but bitter, he may yet think it to be borne.
If he be a true Christian he may say, "I have received the cross, I have received it at Thy hands ;
I will bear it, and bear it till death, as Thou hast
laid it upon me."[2] But when to all this *sin* is

---

[1] Shelley, "Lines Written in Deep Dejection on the Shore at
Naples."   [2] *Imitatio Christi.*

added ; when "calamity meets an accusing conscience"; when a man has the sense of wasted
opportunities, the shame of forsaken ideals, the
sting of evil memories, and the plague of polluted
and polluting thoughts ; when, even at the best,
he feels that, in this or that act or phase of his life
he was unloving, ignoble, uncandid, not what he
ought to have been, not what God would have had
him be, ah! to the noble heart is there not sorrow,
is there not anguish here ?   Apart from deeper and
darker errors, is there not the sense we all must have
of duties unfulfilled; of holy things neglected ; " of
days wasted for ever ; of affections in ourselves or
others trifled with ; of light within turned to darkness " ?   Ah ! when, with our souls, the treacherous
dealers have dealt treacherously, yea, the treacherous
dealers have dealt very treacherously, and we have
been the worst treacherous dealers to ourselves, does
life seem worth having then ?   Should we not say,

> " Alas for man if this were all,
> And nought beyond, oh earth "?

7. So that, when I look at life I say, " Lead, lead me on, my hopes ! "

But if you ask me whether life without God in the world, and with no hope beyond, is worth having, I answer, *No !* nor is it I only who say it, but all the best, and greatest, and wisest of mankind. Ask the kings and queens, ask the poets and scholars, ask the warriors and statesmen, whose dust lies buried here ! Was Elizabeth happy ? was Chatham happy? was Spenser happy ? was even Newton happy ? Ah no ! Over the volumes of human history is written, " Vanity of vanities ! " and the volumes of Biography are full of lamentation and moaning and woe. Scripture itself is a record of human sorrow. I am well aware that they who would rob us of all our hopes; who would take away our Lord out of the sepulchre, so that we know not where they have laid Him ; who would change our God into a struggle of careless forces or a complexity of impersonal laws; who would turn all creation for us into a mask with no living

face behind it, or a hollow eyesocket in which no
eye of love or mercy ever shone—I know that they
tell us that all this makes no difference, and offer
us, for God, I know not what goddess of humanity ;
and I know not what " posthumous activity," for a
life beyond the grave.   My brethren, if they want
to take our fine gold from us, we want no dross or
tinfoil in its place ; nor for the diamonds of heaven
will we take glass and paste.   Some of us at least
will cling to duty, though duty be robbed of all
her sanctions, and to virtue, though virtue lose
every shadow of her reward. We do no need these
sham gods and mock eternities ; and as for the world,
if religion fail to save it from wickedness, God only
knows   what   atheism will do.   It will   not be
content with lacquer religions and pinchbeck faiths.
It will go its way, picking and stealing, chambering
and wantoning, lying and slandering, till the pit
swallow it ; and the sole logical result of scepticism
is that which is openly proclaimed by the cory-
phæus of materialism, the deification of suicide,

the end of evil and futile misery by the extinction and annihilation of the human race.[1]

8. But oh, my brethren, if you will listen to me for a moment more, how, when it is touched by one ray out of God's eternity, does this blank materialism,—this grotto of icicles in the Valley of the Shadow of Death,—melt into mud and nothingness! How does this glaring metal colossus, with its golden head of intellectualism, tumble into impotency when the rock of faith smites it on its feet of miry clay! If there be no hope, and no God, and no things unseen, if there be no atonement for the intolerable wrong, if praying nations uplift their hands in vain, if only a hollow echo followed Christ's prayer of agony upon the Cross, then, as far as I can see, life is a revolting nullity and a hideous dream which no poetic make-believes can redeem from its intolerable weariness. But let but one whisper of God's voice thrill the deafened sense; let but

[1] Schopenhauer.

one gleam of His countenance flash on the blinded
eyes; let His hand hold forth to us but one green
leaf from the Tree of Life; and how is all
changed! Ah, how can we then thank God for
our creation, preservation, and all the blessings
of this life! How can we cry then with bursts
of exultation, " Thou, O God, art our Father, our
Saviour, our merciful God ; and we that are Thy
people and the sheep of Thy pasture will give
Thee thanks for ever." If our thoughts have
come to us this afternoon "clothed in a cloud,"
let them depart "encircled with a rainbow." That
rainbow may seem at times to be but a watery
image, yet it arches the spray of the cataract,
it shines upon the menace of the storm. Sorrows ?
Yes, but to us they are but mercies in disguise.
Sins ? Ah, yes! But they are forgiven and cast
away. Is life worth living ? Ask the atheist,
and if he tells you his real thought it must be
that of the Greek poet " That it were best never
to have been born, and next best to depart as

soon as possible ;"[1] or that of the English
poet :—

> " Count o'er the joys thine hours have seen,
>   Count o'er thy days from anguish free ;
> And know, whatever thou hast been,
>   'Tis something better not to be."

But ask the Christian, "Is life worth living?"
and he will answer, ay, indeed, life is infinitely
worth living, and death is even infinitely more
worth dying ; for to live is Christ, and to die is
gain : to live is to have faith in God, and to die
is to be with Him for evermore.

> " Death is the veil which they who live call life ;
> We sleep, and it is lifted."

---

[1] Soph. *Œd. Col.* 1224 :—

> μὴ φῦναι τὸι ὅπαντα νι-
> κᾷ λόγον · τὸ δ' ἐπεὶ φανῇ
> βῆναι κεῖθεν ὅθενπερ ἥ-
> κει πολὺ δεύτρον, ὡς τάχιστα.

"Non nasci homini longe optumum esse, proxumum autem quam
primum mori."—Cic. *Tusc. Disp.* i. 48, 114 ; cf. Alexis, *Com.* 3,
p. 447. This was indeed one of the commonest sentiments of the
Greeks and Romans, whose life it is the fashion to represent as so
natural and so happy. It was in fact the grand revelation of the im-
prisoned Silenus. See IIdt. viii. 138 ; Aristot. ap. Plut. *Consol.* § 27 ;
Theogn. 543, ap. Welcker, p. 31 ; Creuzer, *Studien.* i. 224. &c.

SERMON III.

"HELL"—WHAT IT IS NOT.[1]

I PET. iv. 6.

" For for this cause was the gospel preached also to them that are dead."

WHEN I spoke from this place last Sunday on the question, " Is life worth living ? " when I preached three Sundays ago on Heaven, some of you may possibly have thought, This is all very well for true Christians ; all very well if in this world there were only saints ; but the saints are few in number, and this world is full of sinners. See what a spectacle it presents ! Look at the coarseness and foulness exhibited at every turn in the streets around us. Walk at night in squalid purlieus, not

[1] Preached in Westminster Abbey, Nov. 11.

E

a stone's throw from this Abbey, where glaring gin-palaces are busy, and amid the reck of alcohol you may hear snatches of foul oaths and odious songs; where women sit shuddering in wretched garrets, to think of the brutal hands which will strike, at the brutal feet that will kick them, when the drunkard staggers home; where the young lads of the schools over which we spend so many millions of money are being daily ruined and depraved by being allured into low haunts of gambling and degradation.   Or walk in the thronged haunts of *commerce*, where myriads are utterly and recklessly absorbed in that hasting to be rich which shall not be innocent ; or judge from the vile phases of the stage and the opera, that vice in higher places is none the less dangerous from being gilded and perfumed ; note all these facts—you may say—and then tell us, not in an ideal world, but in this world, which looks too often as though it were a world without souls—in this world where there is so much of cruel selfishness, of degraded

purpose, of serpentine malice, of insane desire ;—tell
us, in such a world as this, how does all that you
have said apply ?   Alas ! the vast majority of men
and women whom we see are not saints but sinners,
and contented with their sins, and living in their
sins ; and covetousness, and drunkenness, and lust,
and lying, and dishonesty, and hatred, claim each
their multitude of votaries and of victims.   Have
you then any right to paint the world in rose-
colour ? Is it not mere insincerity, mere clericalism,
to shut your eyes to patent facts ?   We, who, by
our very presence here, show that we do not belong
to classes openly and flagrantly irreligious, are yet,
many of us, great sinners.   Even when there is no
dread crime upon our consciences, many of us are
far from God ; our hearts are stained through and
through by evil passions ; we are tied and bound
with the chain of our sins.   You bid us repent ; but
how many do repent ?   You the clergy, who stand
often by the bedsides of the dying ; you who know
how men live, and know that in nine cases

E 2

out of ten they die as they have lived—if your
theory of life is to be complete,—if it is not to be a
mere hollow professional sham—what do you think
about the future ?   Tell us about the lost !

2. My brethren, you have the fullest right to ask
these questions, and it is our bounden duty to
answer them : and I for one—in all deep humility
—yet, now and always asking God for fearless
courage and perfect honesty—will try to give you
such answer as I can.   If it be but the fragment
of an answer, it is because I believe it to be God's
will that no other should be possible ; but at least I
shall strive to speak such truth as is given me to
see, and to answer no man according to his idols.
Those who take loose conjectures for established
certainties ; those who care more for authority than
for reason and conscience ; those who pretend to
dignify with the name of Scriptural argument the
"ever-widening spirals" of dim and attenuated
inference out of " the narrow aperture of single
texts" ; those who talk with the self-complacency

of an ignorance that takes itself for knowledge, as
though they alone had been admitted into what—
with unconscious heresy and unintentional irrever-
ence—they call " the council-chambers of the
Trinity,"—*they* may be ready with glaring and abhorrent pictures of fire and brimstone ; and those
of them who are not tender, and not true, may feel
the consolatory glow of personal security, as they
dilate upon the awfulness and the finality of the
sufferings of the damned.   But those whose faith
must have a broader basis than the halting reconciliation of ambiguous and opposing texts ; they
who grieve at the dark shadows flung by human
theologians athwart God's light ; they who believe
that reason, and conscience, and experience, as
well as Scripture, are books of God, which must
have a direct voice in these great decisions ;[1] they
will not be so ready to snatch God's thunder into

[1] Luke xii. 57, " Yea, and why even of yourselves judge ye not
what is right?"   Prov. xx. 27, "The spirit of man is the candle of
the Lord."   Rom. ii. 14, 15.   "Reason is the only faculty whereby
we have to judge of anything, even revelation itself."—BP. BUTLER.

their own wretched and feeble hands; they will lay
their mouths in the dust, rather than make sad the
hearts which God hath not made sad; they will
take into account the grand principles which domi-
nate through Scripture no less than its isolated
expressions; and undeterred by the base and
feeble notion that virtue would be impossible
without the horrors of an endless hell, they will
declare their *hope* and *trust*—if it be not permitted us to go so far in this matter as belief
and confidence—that, even after death, through
the infinite mercy of the loving Father, many of
the dead shall be alive again and the lost be
found.

3. I cannot pretend, my brethren, to exhaust in
one sermon a question on which whole volumes
have been written. There are some of the young
in this congregation; many of you, I regret to
see, are standing—I am reluctant ever to trespass
too long on your attention, and cannot therefore
profess to-day to meet and to silence all objections.

But one thing I can do—which is to tell you plainly what, after years of thought on this subject, I believe; and what I know to be the belief of multitudes, and of yearly increasing multitudes, of the wisest and most learned both of the laity and of the clergy in our English Church.

4. What the popular notion of hell is, you, my brethren, are all aware. Many of us were scared with it, horrified with it, perhaps almost maddened by it in our childhood. It is that, the moment a human being dies—at whatever age, under whatever disadvantages—his fate is sealed hopelessly and for ever; and that if he die in unrepented sin, that fate is a never-ending agony, amid physical tortures the most frightful that can be imagined; so that, when we think of the future of the human race, we must conceive of "a vast and burning prison, in which the lost souls of millions and millions writhe and shriek for ever, tormented in a flame that never will be

quenched."[1] You have only to read the manuals,
you have only to study the pictures published,
though but rarely, by members of our own Church,
and more frequently by some Roman Catholics
on the one hand, and some sections of Nonconformists on the other,[2] to see that such has been

[1] Rev. S. Cox, *Salvator Mundi*, p. 41. Without entirely agreeing
with Mr. Cox, I can strongly recommend this lucid and forcible argument to all earnest inquirers. It comes with all the greater force
from the author of the *Expositor's Note-Book* and other valuable
works which have thrown a flood of light on the difficulties of
Scripture.

[2] It is quite true that many of the ablest and most thoughtful
Nonconformists—and especially among the vigorous and eloquent
Independent ministers—have rejected the dogma of endless agony
for *all* who die in sin. Nevertheless it is true, I think—though I do
not allude to it in any unkind spirit—that since, as a body, the rank
and file of Roman Catholic priests and Nonconformist ministers are
less highly educated than the Anglican clergy, horrible inventions
about hell—pardonable to the unenlightened mediæval theology, but
not so pardonable now—are to be found with far greater frequency in
the religious literature which originates outside the Anglican Church
than in that which proceeds from within its pale. It is, however,
only just to add that, for Roman Catholics, the pressing and immediate horror of hell is very greatly mitigated, and even to some
degree dispelled, by the doctrine of purgatory. But, alas! pictures of hell which curdle the blood with horror, and thrill the
soul with indignation, are not peculiar to any age, and passages of

and is the *common* belief of Christendom.[1] You
know how Dante, in his vision, comes to a dark
wall of rock, and sees—blacker in the blackness

Tertullian (*De Poenit.* c. 12) and Minucius Felix (*Octav.* 35), or the
Elucidarium usually printed with the works of St. Anselm, are as
frightfully blasphemous against the God of love as those in the *Contemplation of the State of Man* erroneously ascribed to Jeremy
Taylor, or in the tracts of the Rev. J. Furniss or of Mr. Moody.
With these, in charity, I will not stain my page ; but specimens of
them may be seen in Mr. Lecky's *History of Rationalism* (i. 235-
241), where he refers also to Wright's *Purgatory of St. Patrick*,
Delapierre's *L'Enfer décrit par ceux qui l'ont vu*, and Alger's *History of the Doctrine of a Future Life*. Whose heart would not burn
within him with a feeling very opposite to that of love or holiness
after reading such passages ? Nor must it be supposed that in modern
days at least such descriptions have been confined to the sermons of
uneducated people. To avoid giving needless offence in proving
this, I will confine myself to one extract from Jonathan Edwards :—
" The world will probably (!) be converted into a great lake or
liquid globe of fire, in which the wicked shall be overwhelmed,
which shall always be in tempest, in which they shall be tossed to
and fro, having no rest day or night, vast waves or billows of fire
continually rolling over their heads, of which they shall ever be full
of a quick sense, within and without ; their heads, their eyes, their
tongues, their hands, their feet, their loins and their vitals shall for
ever be full of a glowing, melting fire, enough to melt the very rocks
and elements. Also they shall be full of the most quick and lively
sense to feel the torments, not for ten millions of ages, but for ever
and ever, without any end at all," &c., &c.

[1] See Excursus I., Popular Views of Hell.

—the chasm of hell's colossal portal, and, over it, in characters of gloom, the awful line :—

"All hope abandon ye who enter here ;"

and how, passing through it they reach a place, where, in the mere vestibule, and even before they reach the region of more frightful agonies, sighs and wailings trembled through the starless void, and the sound of voices deep and hoarse, and hands smitten wildly together, whirling always through that stained and murky air.[1] But it is

---

[1] " Per me si va nellà citta dolente ;
        Per me si va nell' eterno dolore :
        Per me si va tra la perduta gente.
        *   *   *   *
    Dinanzi a me non fur cose create,
        Se non eterne ed io eterno duro ;
        Lasciate ogni speranza voi ch' entrate.
        *   *   *   *
    Quivi sospiri, pianti, e ad alti guai
        Risonavan per l' aer senza stelle. . . .
        *   *   *   *
    Diverse lingue, orribili favelle,
        Parole di dolore, accenti d' ira
        Voci alti e fioche, e suon di man con elle
    Facevano un tumulto, il qual s' aggira
        Sempre in quell' aria senza tempo tinta,
        Come la rena quando il turbo spira."
                                DANTE, *Infern.*

even more awful to find such things in our own
great writers, who had no belief, like Dante, in that
"willing agony" of purgatory, into which poor
souls might gladly plunge, assured that at last,
redeemed and purified, they too should pass into
their paradisal rest.[1] Read how the great Milton,

[1] Few can estimate the diminution of the horror of contemplating the future which Roman Catholics derive from the doctrine of
purgatory. The souls in purgatory are, as Dante says, " *Contenti
nel fuoco*," and the description in Newman's *Dream of Gerontius*
is that of an agony akin to bliss—

> " Softly and gently, dearly ransomed soul,
>   In my most loving arms I now enfold thee,
> And o'er the pearly waters as they roll
>   I poise thee, and I lower thee, and hold thee ;
> And carefully I dip thee in the lake,
>   And thou, without a sob or a resistance,
> Dost through the flood thy rapid passage take,
>   Sinking deep, deeper into the dim distance."

The antiquity and wide spread of the doctrine of purgatory is
due, in some measure, to the relief which it offered to the conscience
from the dogma against which it revolts.   I do not hold it—a hope
for the future of many of the lost being something very different,
and indeed not necessarily more than the well-known doctrine of
" Mitigatio," and " refrigeria," admitted even by St. Augustine
and St. Jerome.   But the English Church, while in rejecting purgatory it intended to reject any definite belief about a penal state
between death and judgment, in which souls are purified by pains

after telling us of "the supereminence of beatific
vision," plunges at once into the frightful sentence
that they who have been wicked in high places,
"after a shamefull end in this life (which God
grant them), shall be thrown downe eternally
into the deepest and darkest gulfe of hell, where
under the despightfull controule, the trample and
spurn of all the other damned, that, in the anguish
of their torture, shall have no other ease than to
exercise a raving and bestiall tryanny over them
as their slaves and negroes, they shall remaine in
that plight for ever,—the basest, the lowermost,
the most dejected, most underfoot and downe-
trodden vassals of perdition."[1]   Or read Bishop
Jeremy Taylor's sermon on Christ's Advent to
Judgment, and see how his imagination revels in
the "Tartarean drench" which he pours over his
lurid page, when he tells us how "God's heavy
hand shall press the *sanies* and the intolerableness,

which may be abbreviated by prayer and masses, did not close the
door of hope, and most deliberately refrained from doing so.

   [1] Milton, *Of Reformation in England*, ii. *ad. fin.*

the obliquity, and the unreasonableness, the amazement and the disorder, the smart and the sorrow,
the guilt and the punishment, out from all our
sins, and pour them into one chalice, and mingle
them with an infinite wrath, and make the wicked
drink off all the vengeance, and force it down
their unwilling throats, with the violence of devils
and accursed spirits." [1]   Or, once more, read in

---

[1] Jeremy Taylor, *Works*, viii. 24 (Eden's edition).   Here is
another specimen :—" For though in hell the accursed souls shall
have no worse than they have deserved, and there are not these over-
running measures as there are in heaven, and therefore that the joys
of heaven are infinitely greater joys than the pains of hell are great
pains, yet even these are a full measure to a full iniquity, pain above
patience, sorrow without ease, amazement without consideration,
despair without the intervals of a little hope, indignation without
the possession of any good ; there dwells envy and confusion, disorder and sad remembrances, perpetual woes and continual shriek-
ings, uneasiness, and all the evils of the soul."—*Id.* p. 39.

What a world, we may well exclaim, for the loving and merciful
eye of God to contemplate !   How frightful a result, in spite of how
infinite a sacrifice !   And we are taught that one instant makes all
the difference between a poor, frail, sinful soul, over which its
Saviour yearns, for which the Spirit pleads, which God, its Father
and Creator, loves with an infinite tenderness, and a lost, accursed,
shrieking, blaspheming, ever-never-dying son of endless and irre-
trievable perdition !   This is what the popular, the common view

Henry Smith—the silver-tongued Platonist of Cambridge—how, when Iniquity hath played her part, " all the Furies of Hell leap upon the man's heart, like a stage.—Thought calleth to Fear ; Fear whistleth to Horror ; Horror beckoneth to Despair, and saith, ' Come and help me torment this sinner.' . . Irons are laid upon his body, like a prisoner. All his lights are put out at once."[2] Can we wonder that, receiving and believing such doctrines, the poet Habington writes :—

> " Fix me on some bleake precipice,
>   Where I ten thousand years may stand,

has a thousand times asserted, and still professes to assert ! . . And is this the Gospel ? Are these the "glad tidings of great joy?"

Yet Jeremy Taylor, who as I have pointed out in *Masters of English Theology*, p. 195), not unfrequently uses wavering language, seems to have held the theory of conditional immortality,—at any rate, as Coleridge observes, *in abditis fidei*. For, after observing in this same sermon (*Works*, viii. p. 43), that this was the belief of Justin Martyr, and of Irenæus, and noticing different fancies of the Fathers on this subject, he refers to the argument that " though the fire is everlasting, not all that enters into it is everlasting," and that the word "everlasting" "signifies only to the end of its proper period."

[1] Sermon on the Betraying of Christ.

> Made now a statua of ice,
>   Then by the summer scorch'd and tann'd !
> Place me alone in some fraile boate
>   'Mid th' horrours of an angry sea ;
> Where I, while time shall move, may floate,
>   Despairing either land or day :
> Or, under earth my youth confine
>   To th' night and silence of a cell,
> Where scorpions may my limbs entwine,
>   O God ! so Thou forgive me hell ! " [1]

or that Shakspeare, after lines of marvellous power,
should exclaim—

>   " 'Tis too horrible ;
> The weariest and most loathèd earthly life
> Which age, ache, penury, and imprisonment
> Can lay on nature, is a paradise
> To what we fear of death ! " [2]

5. Well, my brethren, happily the thoughts and
hearts of men are often far gentler and nobler
than the formulæ of their creeds ; and custom and
tradition prevent even the greatest from facing
the full meaning and consequences of the words
they use.

When Milton talks thus of Hell he is but giving

---

[1] Habington's *Castara*.   [2] *Measure for Measure*, iii. 1.

form and colour to his burning hatred of irresistible tyranny and triumphant wrong; when
Jeremy Taylor and other great divines and poets
wrote thus of it, they gave us but the ebullient
flashes from the glowing caldron of a kindled
imagination.[1] What they say is but, as it were,
the poetry of indignation. It is only when these
topics fall into vulgar handling,—it is only when
they reek like acrid fumes from the poisoned
crucible of mean and loveless conceptions,—that
we see them in all their intolerable ghastliness.
Many true and loving Christians have, I know,
held these views, and have mourned with aching
hearts over what seemed to them the fatal necessity for believing them.[2] But others, less good
and less pure, have *exulted* in them, and I know
nothing more calculated to make the whole soul
revolt with loathing from every doctrine of religion

[1] See Coleridge, *Apologetic Preface to Fire, Famine, and
Slaughter.*

[2] Excursus II., 'Agony of Christians in Contemplating the
Doctrine of Endless Torments.'

than the evil complacency with which some cheer-
fully accept the belief that they are living and
moving in the midst of millions doomed irreversibly to everlasting perdition.   St. Augustine
dared to say that infants dying unbaptised would
certainly be damned, though only with a *levissima
damnatio*.[1]   Even St. Thomas of Aquinum lent his

---

[1] " Potest recte dici parvulos sine baptismo de corpore exeuntes
in damnatione omnium mitissimo futuros."—August. *De peccat.
meritis et remiss.* i. 16 ; *Enchirid.* 93.   He condemned the
Pelagian doctrine of a *limbus infantum.*   "Non est ullus ulli
medius locus, *ut possit esse* nisi cum diabolo, qui non est cum
Christo." *De peccat. merit.* i. 28.   See Hagenbach, *Hist. of Doc-.*
trines, i. 390 (English translation).

Owing mainly to the authority of St. Augustine, which was in
many respects so disastrous, the entire Mediæval Church held the
doctrine of the damnation of infants dying unbaptised.   Dante, in
the first circle of the *Inferno*, sees the

> " Duol senza martiri,
> Ch' avean le turbe, ch' eran molte e grandi
> E d'*infanti* e di femmine e di viri,"

of which the Master, himself a sufferer in that limbo, says—

> " Per tai difetti, e non per altrio rio
> Semo perduti, e sol di tanto offesi
> Che senza speme vivemo i disio,"

i.e. " without hope, we live in desire " of seeing God.   *Inf.* iv,
28—43.   Comp. *Paradise Lost*, x. 995.

F

saintly name to what I can only call the abomin-
able fancy that the bliss of the saved may be
all the more keen because they are permitted to
gaze on the punishment of the wicked.[1] Boston,
in his *Fourfold State*, talks of God holding up the

---

[1] "Unumquodque ex comparatione contrarii magis cognoscitur
. . . et ideo ut beatitudo sanctorum eis magis complaceat, et de ea
uberiores gratias Deo agant, datur eis ut poenam impiorum perfecte
videant !"—St. Thom. Aquin. *Summa Theol.* iii. Suppl. Qu. 94.
art. I.

Compare the language of Peter Lombard :—"Egredientur ergo
electi ad vivendum impiorum cruciatus, quos videntes *non dolore
afficientur, sed laetitia satiabuntur,* visâ impiorum ineffabili calami-
tate."—*Sentent.* iv. dist. 5, 9.

Strange influence of system and dogma ! Can any one with a
heart, any man worthy of the name of Christian, any man worthy
of the name of man, fully realise the meaning of such words with
a soul unblinded by prejudice and unsteeled by custom, without
calling it *inhuman* language, and wondering that any could have
uttered it who thought that they were preaching a gospel of infinite
love ?

Yet *even this* has survived to us from the Middle Ages.

"The damned," wrote Jonathan Edwards, "shall be tormented
in the presence of the holy angels, and in the presence of the Lamb,
so will they be tormented also in the presence of the glorified saints.
Hereby the saints will be made more sensible how great their salvation is. *The view of the misery of the damned will double the ardour
of the love and gratitude of the saints in heaven.*"

wicked in hell-fire with the one hand, and tor-
menting them with the other.   Now even a saint
of God sins when he speaks thus, and is setting up
in the place of God the Idol of the Tribe or of
the Den, and no language can be stern enough
to reprobate the manner in which some, who are
not saints of God at all, who are not even the
elder brothers of the Prodigal, whose religion has re-
solved itself into a mere feeble heresy-hunting, have
turned God's gospel of plenteous redemption into
an anathema of all but universal perdition.   Which
of us has not heard sermons, or read books to the
effect that if every leaf of the forest trees, and every
grain of the ocean sands stood for billions of
years, and all these billions were exhausted, you
would still be no nearer even to the beginning of
eternity than at the first ;[1] and that (pardon me for

[1] One specimen—neither more nor less futile than hundreds of
others—will suffice.   " Give us a millstone," say the damned, "as
large as the whole earth, and so wide in circumference as to touch
the sky all round, and let a little bird come once in a hundred thou.
sand years and pick off a small particle of the stone not larger than
the tenth part of a grain of millet, and after another hundred

F 2

reproducing what I abhor) if you could conceive
an everlasting toothache, or an endless cautery,
or the incessant scream of a sufferer beneath the
knife, that would give you but a faint conception
of the agony of hell ; and yet in the same breath
that the majority of mankind are doomed to hell
by an absolute predestination ? Which of us has
not heard teaching which implied, or did not even
shrink from stating this ? And dare any one of
you regard such teaching as other than blasphemy

thousand years let him come again, so that in ten hundred thousand
years he would pick off as much as a grain of millet ; we wretched
sinners would desire nothing but that thus the stone might have an
end, and thus our pains also : yet even that cannot be !"—Suso
(died 1365).

" O cӕcas hominum mentes !"

But are we really bidden to believe that after a life sad and
troubled as most of our lives are, man with his judgment so weak,
his passions so strong, his temptations so intense, shall after a few
years be tortured by a merciful, long-suffering God, "not only
millions of years of pain for each thought, or word, or act of sin
. . . not only millions of ages only for every such act, but a punishment which *when millions of ages of judgment have been inflicted for
every moment man has lived on earth is no nearer its end than when
it first commenced ?* "—See Mr. Jukes's excellent book, *The Restitution of All Things*, p. 115.

against the merciful God ?   If you are not un-
affected when "the destitute perish of hunger, or
the dying agonise in pain," is there any human
being, worthy the dignity of a human being, whose
soul does not revolt and sicken at the notion of
"a world all worm and flame"?   One who is not
of us wrote yesterday to the *Times*, how, standing in that Parisian prison where the Girondists
held their last supper ; whence Danton passed to
his scaffold ; where Robespierre, the night before
his execution, lay weltering in his blood ; where
Marie Antoinette poured out her soul in the last
hour of her life ; he saw an exquisite crucifix of
ivory in the cell where it had been left since that
queen, and wife, and mother had turned to it all
night in her last agony ; and he adds that, in such
a scene as that, all logic, doctrine, politics, severity
of judgment are hushed, and "Human nature
asserts its preëminence, and claims the whole field
of thought for pity.   In presence of that agonising
figure on the cross, the whole soul revolts against

judicial terrorism in whatsoever name, by whatsoever tyrant committed." He is speaking, of
course, of earthly tyrants; but, my brethren,
"Shall not the Judge of all the earth do right?"
and shall the image of the crucified Redeemer
inspire, in one who rejects His divinity, the noble
pity which seems as if it were alien to many of
His sons? I can sympathise with the living poet
when he cries,—

> " Were it not thus, O King of my salvation,
>   Many would curse to Thee, and I for one,
> Fling Thee Thy bliss, and snatch at Thy damnation,
>   Scorn and abhor the shining of the sun ;
> Ring with a reckless shivering of laughter,
>   Wroth at the woe which Thou hast seen so long,
> Question if any recompense hereafter
>   Waits to atone the intolerable wrong."

If St. Paul, again and again, flings from him
with a "God forbid!" the conclusions of an ap-
parently irresistible logic,[1] we surely, who have
very little logic of any kind against us in this

---

[1] See an admirable sermon on the subject preached at Oxford by
my friend Prof. Plumptre.

matter, but only questionable exegesis, supported
in too many instances by spiritual selfishness and
impenetrable prejudice,—do in the high name of
the outraged conscience of humanity,—nay, in
the far higher names of the God who loves, of
the Saviour who died for, of the Spirit who
enlightens us,—hurl from us representations so
cruel, of a doctrine so horrible, with every nerve
and fibre of our intellectual, moral, and spiritual
life.[1] Ignorance may make a fetish of such a
doctrine if it will; Pharisaism may inscribe it
upon its phylacteries; hatred may write it,

---

[1] My language in this, and in the preceding and subsequent para-
graphs, has been either intentionally perverted or unintentionally
misunderstood. I apply these terms (strong, if you will, but not, it
seems to me, in the slightest degree too strong), *not* of course to the
general belief in endless punishment, but *to the awful variations
upon it, and inventions about it*, to which I have referred. Many,
I know, who are blessed and holy souls, believe, or imagine themselves to believe, in an endless hell for most of the human race ; but
when they in any way *face the significance of their own words* the
language which they use is that of the authors adduced in Excursus
II., not that of those referred to in Excursus III. "On the Popular
Views of Hell."

instead of " Holiness to the Lord," on the sacerdotal *petalon* in which it degrades and simulates the name of love :—but here, in this vast mausoleum of the glorious dead, here amid the silent memorials of the sons of fame and the fathers who begat us, of whom many, though not saints, were yet noble, though erring men ;— and of whom (though they, and we alike, shall suffer, both here and hereafter, the penalty of unrepentant sin) we yet cannot and will not think as damned to unutterable tortures by irreversible decrees,—I repudiate these crude and glaring travesties of the awful and holy will of God ; I arraign them as ignorantly merciless ; I impeach them as a falsehood against Christ's universal and absolute redemption ; I denounce them as a blasphemy against God's exceeding and eternal love ! And more acceptable, I am very sure, than the rigidest and most uncompromising self-styled orthodoxy of all the Pharisees who have ever judged their brethren since time

began—more acceptable by far to Him, the friend
of publicans and sinners, who, on His cross, prayed
for His murderers, and who died that we might
live—more acceptable, I say, by far, than the
delight which amid a deluge of ruin hugs itself
upon the plank which it has seized—would be
the noble and trembling pity—so fearfully unlike
the language of divines and schoolmen,—which
made St. Paul ready to be anathema from
Christ for the sake of his brethren ;[1] which
made Moses cry to His God at Sinai, " Oh, this
people have sinned : and now, if Thou wilt forgive
their sin—; and if not, blot me, I pray Thee, out of
Thy book which Thou hast written." [2]

6. But I would ask you to believe, my brethren,
that I speak now no longer with natural passion,
but with most accurate theological precision, when
I say that, though texts may be quoted which give
primâ facie plausibility to such modes of teaching,
yet, to say nothing of the fact that the light and.

---

[1] Rom. ix. 3.   [2] Ex. xxxii. 32.

love which God Himself has kindled in us recoil from them,—those texts are, in the first place, alien to the broad unifying principles of Scripture ;—that they are founded on interpretations which have appeared to many wise men to be demonstrably groundless ;—and that for every one so quoted, two can be adduced whose *primâ facie* and literal interpretation tells on the other side.[1] There is an old, sensible, admitted rule, " Theologia symbolica *non est* demonstrativa "—in other words, that phrases which belong to metaphor, to imagery, to poetry, to emotion, are not to be formulated into necessary dogma, or crystallised into rigid creed. Tested by this rule, nine-tenths of the phrases on which these views are built fall utterly to the ground. But even were this otherwise, yet, once more, in the name of Christian light and Christian liberty ;—once more in the name of Christ's promised Spirit ;—once more in

[1] See Excursus IV. Texts bearing on the doctrine of Eternal Hope.

the name of the broadened dawn, and the daystar
which has arisen in our hearts ;—I protest at once
and finally against this ignorant tyranny of isolated
texts which has ever been the curse of Christian
truth, the glory of narrow intellects, and the cause
of the worst errors of the worst days of the corrupted Church. Tyranny has engraved texts
upon her sword ; Oppression has carved texts
upon her fetters; Cruelty has tied texts around
her faggots; Ignorance has set knowledge at de-
fiance with texts woven on her flag. Gin-drinking
has been defended out of Timothy, and slavery
has made a stronghold out of Philemon. The
devil, as we all know, can quote texts for his
purpose. They were quoted by the Pharisees,
not once or twice only, against our Lord Himself,
and when St. Paul fought the great battle of
Christian freedom against the curse of Law, he was
anathematised with a whole Pentateuch of opposing texts. But we, my brethren, are in the dispensation of the Holy Spirit. Our guide is the

Scriptures of God in their broad outlines;—the
Revelation of God in its glorious unity;—the
Books of God in their eternal simplicity, read by
the illumination of that Spirit of Christ which
dwelleth in us, except we be reprobates.[1] Our
guide is not, and never shall be, what the Scriptures call "the letter that killeth;"[2]—the tyrannous realism of ambiguous metaphors, the asserted
infallibility of isolated words. But if this must
be made simply and solely a matter of texts;—
if, except as a dead anachronism, we mean nothing
when we say, "I believe in the Holy Ghost!"—
if we prefer our sleepy shibboleths and dead
traditions to the living promise, "I will dwell in
them and walk in them;"—then by all means let
this question be decided by texts alone. I am
quite content that texts should decide it. Only,
first, you must go to the inspired original, not to the
erroneous translation; and *secondly*, you must take

---

[1] 2 Cor. xiii. 5.
[2] 2 Cor. iii. 6; Rom. ii. 29; vii. 6; John vi. 63.

words, and interpret words in their proper and his-
torical significance, not in that sense which makes
them connote to you a thousand notions which did
not originally belong to them; and *thirdly*, you
must not explain away, or read between the lines
of the texts which make against the traditional
view, while you refuse all limitation of those on
the misinterpretation or undue extension of which
that view is founded. Now I ask you, my brethren,
where would be these popular teachings about hell
—the kind of teachings which I have quoted to you
and described—if we calmly and deliberately, by
substituting the true translations, erased from our
English Bibles, as being inadequate or erroneous or
disputed renderings, the three words, " damnation,"
"hell," and "everlasting"? Yet I say, unhesitatingly,
—I say, claiming the fullest right to speak on this
point,—I say, with the calmest and most unflinch-
ing sense of responsibility,—I say, standing here
in the sight of God, and of my Saviour, and it
may be of the angels and spirits of the dead—

that not one of those three expressions ought to
stand any longer in our English Bibles, and that,
being—in our present acceptation of them—in the
notion (that is) which all uneducated persons
attach to them—simply *mistranslations*, they most
unquestionably will not stand unexplained in the
revised version of the Bible if the revisers have
understood their duty.[1]   The verb "to damn" in
the Greek Testament is neither more nor less
than the verb "to condemn," and the words translated "damnation" are simply the words which,
in the vast majority of instances the same translators have translated, and rightly translated, by
"judgment" and "condemnation."   The word
αἰώνιος, sometimes translated "everlasting," is
simply the word which, in its first sense, means
agelong or *æonian;* and which is in the Bible
itself applied to things which have utterly and
long since passed away; and is in its second sense

---

[1] See Excursus V. On the translation of κρίνειν, αἰώνιος, and
Γεέν.α.

something "spiritual"—something above and beyond time,—as when the knowledge of God is said to be eternal life.[1] So that when, with your futile billions, you foist into this word αἰώνιος the fiction of endless time, you do but give the lie to the mighty oath of that great angel, who set one foot upon the sea, and one upon the land, and with hand uplifted to heaven sware by Him who liveth for ever and ever that "Time should be no more."[2] And finally in the

[1] See Excursus VI. On the word αἰώνιος.

[2] Rev. x. 7. ὅτι χρόνος οὐκέτι ἔσται. This has been interpreted to mean "That no further delay should intervene." It may possibly be so, but the meaning attached to it by Bede, " Mutabilis sæcularium temporum varietas in novissimâ tubâ cessabit "—which is also the rendering of the E. V.—furnishes a very true and noble sense, the possibility of which is by no means disproved.

> " For spirits and men by different standards mete
> The less and greater in the flow of time.
> *   *   *   *   *
> Not so with us in the immaterial world ;
> But intervals in their succession
> Are measured by the living thought alone,
> And grow or wane with its intensity.
> And time is not a common property,
> But what is long is short, and swift is slow,
> And near is distant, as received and grasped
> By this mind or by that, and every one
> Is standard of his own chronology."
>   NEWMAN, *Dream of Gerontius.*

Gospels and Epistles the word rendered Hell
is in one place the Greek "Tartarus," borrowed
as a name for the prison of evil spirits, not
after, but *until*, the resurrection; in five places
"Hades," which simply means the world beyond
the grave; and in twelve places "Gehenna,"
which means primarily the Valley of Hinnom
outside Jerusalem, in which, after it had been
polluted by Moloch-worship, corpses were flung
and fires were lit; and is used, secondarily, as a
metaphor, not of fruitless and hopeless, but—for
all at any rate but a small and desperate minority
—of that purifying and corrective punishment
which, as all of us alike believe, does await im-
penitents in both here and beyond the grave.

But, be it solemnly observed, the Jews *to* whom
and in whose metaphorical sense, the word was
used by our Blessed Lord, never did, either then,
or at any period, normally attach to the word
Gehenna that meaning of endless torment which
we attach to "Hell." To them, and in their style of

speech,—and therefore on the lips of our blessed Saviour who addressed it to them, and spake in terms which they would understand—it meant *not* a material and everlasting fire, but an intermediate, a remedial, a metaphorical, a terminable retribution.[1]

[1] I call earnest attention to the immense importance of this argument. It surely cannot be denied that our Blessed Lord, speaking as "*Judaeus, ad Judaeos, apud Judaeos*," must have used the words of His day in the sense wherein those words would have been understood by His hearers. If so it is *demonstrable* that the Jews did not hold, and as a Church they never have held, the two doctrines which I am here declaring to be unproven, viz.,

1. The finality of the doom passed at death. The universal and very ancient use by the Jews of the *Kaddish*, or prayer for the dead, is a sufficient proof of this.

2. The doctrine of torment, endless if once incurred.

Neither etymologically nor historically, nor in its ordinary usage, does the word convey that meaning. Gehenna is spoken of some five times, I believe, in the Mishna, and in no one of them does it connote what "Hell" connotes to the common ear. For the original significance of "Gehenna" I may refer to my article on "Hell" in Dr. Smith's *Dictionary of the Bible*. For the meaning attached to it by Jews themselves I may quote the testimony of some very learned Talmudic scholars.

"There is *no everlasting damnation according to the Talmud*. There is only a temporary punishment, even for the worst sinners. 'Generations upon generations' shall last the punishment of

G

7. Thus then, finding nothing in Scripture or any-where to prove that the fate of every man is, at

idolaters, apostates, and traitors. But 'there is a space of only two fingers' breadth between hell and heaven :' the sinner has but to repent sincerely and the gates to everlasting bliss will spring open."—Deutsch, *Remains*, p. 53.

After verifying and examining every passage in the Talmud quoted by Lightfoot, Schöttgen, Buxtorf, Castell, Schindler, Glass, Bartoloccius, Ugolino, and York, Dr. Dewes declares as the result of his examination "that there are but two passages which even a superficial reader could consider to be corroborative of the assertion that the Jews understood Gehenna to be a place of everlasting punishment."—*Plea for a New Translation*, p. 23.

We find such passages as these : "Gehenna is nothing but a day in which the impious shall be burned."—*Abhoda Zara*, i.

"The judgment of the ungodly is for twelve months."—*Adyôth*, ii. 10.

Babha Metzia, 58 ; *Jebhamôth*, 102 ; *Nedarim*, 40, &c.

The editor of the *Jewish Chronicle*—generally believed to be a learned Talmudist—emphatically declares in recent numbers that endless torment has *never* been taught by the Rabbis as a doctrine of the Jewish Church.

"Die Strafen in Gehenna. *In diesem* Punkt erklären sich die Talmudlehrer *entschieden gegen die Annahme der Ewigkeit der Höllenstrafen.*"—Hamburger *Talmudisches Wörterbuch* : s.v. Hölle.

For further testimonies ancient and modern on these very important facts, see pp. 207—214. They are more, than sufficient to prove that the language of the Targums (Jonathan on Is. xxxiii. 14, lxv. 5, Onkelos on Deut. xxxiii. 6, Gfrörer, *Jahrb. des Heil's*, ii. 289, 311) has no bearing on the controversy, since "fire" and

death, irrevocably determined, I shake off the
hideous incubus of atrocious conceptions—I mean

"for ever," mean in them just what they do in Scripture, and no
more.   See Exc. p. 197.   The most distinct utterance in the
Talmud is Rosh Hashand, i. (f. 16, 2, 17, 1), where it is said that
the just shall rise to bliss; ordinary sinners shall be ultimately
redeemed; the hopelessly bad shall be punished for a year, and
then annihilated. (See Buxtorf, *Syndg. Judaica*, p. 23; Eisenmenger,
Entdecktes Judenth. 323—369.   Any one may here see that a year
was the ordinary period fixed by the rabbis to their purgatory.)

We have therefore this result.   If our revisers retain the word
"Hell" for Gehenna they will be perpetuating in the English
word its latest, darkest, and (as I believe) least Scriptural conno-
tations; and will be stereotyping a series of untenable inferences,
by substituting for the technical expression a rendering which
involves conceptions deliberately excluded by those who used the
original word.

*Surely it is a sacred duty in this matter to follow the example
set by Christ and the Apostles themselves.*   When they spoke of
Gehenna they spoke of something to which a definite meaning
was attached; and instead of obscuring that definite meaning by
changing it into some inexact Greek expression, *they simply trans-
ferred the Hebrew term into a Greek transliteration*.   To thousands
of educated men "Hell" and "Gehenna" *must* mean henceforth
different things, and to try to make them equivalent will be a
perpetuation of error which must inevitably doom the work of
the revisers to yet further revision.   In all humility, but with
deep earnestness, feeling how much is at stake, I intreat them to
allow due weight to these considerations.

G 2

those conceptions of unimaginable horror and physical excruciation endlessly prolonged—attached by popular ignorance and false theology to the doctrine of future retribution. But neither can I dogmatise on the other side. I see nothing to prove the distinctive belief attached to the word Purgatory. I cannot accept the spreading doctrine of Conditional Immortality; I cannot preach the certainty of Universalism. That last doctrine—the belief that

> " Good shall fall
> At last, far off, at last to all,"—

does indeed derive much support from many passages of Scripture; it—or a view more or less analogous to it—was held by Origen, the greatest and noblest, by Gregory of Nyssa, the most fearless, by Clemens of Alexandria, the most learned, by Gregory of Nazianzus, one of the most eloquent, by Justin Martyr, one of the earliest of the Fathers; it was spoken of in some places with half approval, or with a rejection which even when

absolute was sympathetic and respectful, by theologians like St. Irenæus, St. Athanasius, St. Jerome,
St. Ambrose, even St. Augustine himself;[1] in
modern times, among many others, it has been
held by great and most orthodox theologians like
Bengel and Tholuck, and by saints of God like
Erskine of Linlathen and Bishop Ewing of Argyll.
And further, whatever may have been the motives
which influenced them, the Reformers struck out
of the Prayer-book the Forty-second Article, which
declared that "All men shall not be saved."[2]   On

[1] For an examination of this statement, see Excursus III. Sketch
of Eschatological opinions.

[2] The excluded Forty-second Article (of 1552) ran as follows :—
" *All men shall not bee saved at the length.*

"Thei also are worthie of condemnation who indeavour at
this time to restore the dangerouse opinion that al menne, be thei
never so ungodlie, shall at length bee saved, when they have suffered
pain for their sinnes a certaine time appointed by God's justice."

It was omitted in 1562, and almost certainly through the influence
of Archbishop Parker.

Now on this Article I observe that if the omission of the
original Forty-first Article left the belief in the millennium open (as
most " Evangelicals " admit), the omission of this Article leaves
even " Universalism " an open question.   But as far as I am

such a question as this I care but little for individual authority, but this much at least is proved
by the many differing theories of wise and holy
men—that God has given us no clear and decisive
revelation on the final condition of those who have
died in sin. It is revealed to us that "God is
love;"[1] and that "Him to know is life eternal;"[2]
and that it is not His will that any should perish;[3]
and that "as in Adam all die, even so in Christ
shall all be made alive;"[4] but how long, even
after death, man may continue to resist His will;—
how long he may continue in that spiritual death
which is alienation from God;—that is one of the
secret things which God hath not revealed. But
this much, at any rate—that the fate of man is not
finally and irreversibly sealed at death, you yourselves—unwittingly perhaps, but none the less

concerned the Article would not have touched my view at all, for
I am not a Universalist.

[1] I John iv. 8.   [2] James xvii. 2.
[3] 2 Pet. iii. 9.   [4] I Cor. xv. 22.

certainly admit, and declare, and confess, every time you repeat, in the Apostles' Creed, that Christ descended into hell. For the sole passage which proves that article of the Creed is the passage in St. Peter, which tells us that " He went and preached to the Spirits in prison,[1] which sometime were disobedient." St. Peter in my text tells you in so many words that "the Gospel was preached to them that were dead," and if, as the Church in every age has held, the fate of *those* dead sinners was not irrevocably fixed by death, then it must be clear and obvious to the meanest understanding that neither of necessity is ours.[2]

There then is the sole answer which I can give to your question, " What about the lost ? " My belief is fixed upon " that living God " who we

[1] That the prisoners there may be " prisoners of hope," appears from Matt. v. 26, where the same word, φυλακή, is used. Even if the payment of the debt be not possible to man it is possible to God (Matt. xix. 26).

[2] See Dr. Plumptre's sermon at St. Paul's, " The Spirits in Prison," of which Bishop Thirlwall spoke in terms of the very warmest approval.

are told is "the Saviour of all men." My answer
is with Thomas Erskine of Linlathen, that "we
are lost here as much as there, and that Christ
came to seek and save the lost;" and my hope
is that the vast majority, at any rate, of the lost,
may at length be *found*. If any hardened sinner,
shamefully loving his sin, and despising the long-
suffering of his Saviour, *trifle* with that doctrine,
it is at his own just and awful peril. But if, on
the other hand, there be some among you—as are
there not?—souls sinful indeed, yet not hard in
sin;—souls that fail indeed, yet even, amid their
failing, long, and pray, and love, and agonise, and
strive to creep ever nearer to the light;—then I say,
Have faith in God. There is hope for you;—hope
for you, even if death overtake you before the final
victory is won;—hope for the poor in spirit, for
theirs is the kingdom of heaven;—hope for the
mourners, for they shall be comforted,—though you
too may have to be purified in that Gehenna of
æonian fire beyond the grave. Yes, my brethren,

" Say ye to the righteous, that it shall be well with him ; for they shall eat the fruit of their doings. Woe unto the wicked ! it shall be ill with him ; for the reward of his hands shall be given him : "[1]— but say also, as Christ's own Apostles said, that there shall be " a restitution of *all* things,"[2]—that God willeth not that *any* should perish ;[3]—that Christ both died, and rose, and revived that He might be Lord both of the dead and the living ;[4]— that as in Adam all die, even so in Christ shall all be made alive ;[5]—and that the day shall come when " *all*[6] things shall be subdued unto Him, that God may be *all in all*"—πάντα ἐν πᾶσιν—omnia in omnibus—*all things in all men.*

---

[1] Is. iii. 10.   [2] Acts iii. 21.
[3] 2 Pet. iii. 9 ; Ezek. xxxiii. 11 ; Ro. ii. 4 ; 1 Tim. ii. 4.
[4] Rom. xiv. 9.   [5] 1 Cor. xv. 22.   [6] 1 Cor. xv. 28.

SERMON IV.

ARE THERE FEW THAT BE SAVED?[1]

LUKE xiii. 23, 24.

"Then said one unto Him, Lord, are there few that be saved?
And He said unto them, Strive to enter in at the strait gate."

THIS passage, my brethren, gives us the very
essence of our Lord's teaching respecting the
present and the future. Since He had dwelt so
often on the difficulty and narrowness of virtue's
uphillward path, and on the few who toil in it,
whereas many are to be seen rushing along the
broad road that leadeth to destruction,—some
one (who perhaps had more speculative curiosity
than moral earnestness) wanted to know the

---

[1] Preached in Westminster Abbey, Nov. 18, 1877.

issues of this fact;—and therefore asked Him the
plain, direct question, "Lord, are there few that
be saved?" Now supposing that it were so;
—supposing that, as thousands of theologians have
taught for thousands of years, the vast majority
are in the next world for ever lost,—would not our
Lord have said so? would not His teaching have
gained a terrific awfulness from admitting it? Had
the answer to the question been a plain "Yes!"
—and had that view been as essential to morality
as some assert,—surely it would have been *worse*
than dangerous,—it would have been *unkind* to
suppress it! But what is the answer of Divine
wisdom? Is it some glaring agony of fire and
brimstone for billions of years? Is it in that
style in which the coarse terrorism of the Puritan
is at one with the coarse terrorism of the Inqui-
sition? No; but it is a refusal to answer. It
is a strong warning to the questioner. It is a
tacit rebuke of the very question. It is the
pointing to a strait gate, and a narrow way,

whereby alone we can enter into the kingdom
of God. In this sad world it is but the few who
find that way, and *until* they find it they cannot
see the kingdom of God. But there is not one
word here about an irreversible doom to a material torment ; not one word to tell us that all
who walk in that broad road inevitably reach its
fatal goal. And are we not ' bound to consider the
silences of Scripture no less than its utterances ? '
If we still yearn for any answer about the future
we may find it perhaps in the glorious words of
Isaiah, " Fear not ; for I am with thee : I will bring
thy seed from the East, and gather thee from the
West ; I will say to the North, Give up ; and to
the South, Keep not back ; bring my sons from
far, and my daughters from the ends of the
earth ;"[1] or in the dazzling vision of the seer of the
Apocalypse, " I beheld, and lo ! a great multitude,
which no man could number, of all nations, and
kindreds, and peoples, and tongues, stood before

[1] Is. xli. 10.

the throne, and before the Lamb, clothed with
white robes, and palms in their hands;"[1] or in
the calm promise of our Blessed Lord Himself.
" In My Father's House are many mansions."[2]
But the spirit of the answer of our Blessed Lord
was this, " The fate of the souls that He hath
made is in the hands of Him that made them, not
in thine. Enter thou in at the strait gate."

2. It was in that spirit, my brethren, that I
strove to speak to you last Sunday, believing that
much of the popular teaching about the awful
subject of future retribution—its physical tortures,
its endless duration, its irreversible finality at the
instant of death,—gives us an utterly false picture
of the God of Love, which, though it may find
warrant in the *primâ facie* aspect of texts wrongly
translated or totally misunderstood, finds no
warrant either in the general tone of Scripture
or in God's no less sacred teachings to our individual souls. And if some would represent such

[1] Rev. vii. 9.   [2] John xiv. 2.

a view as dangerous, I reply that my only question is, 'Is it true?' It is falsehood which is always dangerous; but truth never. It is not for us to construct after our own fashion the unseen world. *You* think that men will not love God without the terror of an endless hell? So thought not David. He said, "There is mercy with Thee : *therefore* shalt Thou be feared." And in any case it is useless to dogmatise about things which God has not revealed. "Things are as they are, and will be as they will be;" and for us to misrepresent them by the fallibility of human system, or at the bidding of human expedience, is a blasphemy against truth and against God. What *is* dangerous is to drive some into indignant atheism, and to entangle others with an evil superstition, and to crush others under a deep despair, by representing.Him whose name is Love as a remorseless Avenger, instead of as a Father, who is gracious and merciful, slow to anger and of great kindness, neither keepeth He His anger for ever. Evil souls

and foolish souls can make any doctrine dangerous.
St. Peter tells us that they wrested the writings
of St. Paul, as they did also the other Scriptures,
to their own destruction ;[1] would you, therefore,
have had the Scriptures unwritten? or ought St.
Paul never to have taken up his pen? Some of the
Fathers, I am afraid, held what I believe to be the
truth on this matter,—just as hundreds of our ablest
clergy do,—but feared to preach it ;[2] but the best

---

[1] 2 Pet. iii. 16.

[2] Origen (*C. Cels.* vi. 26) openly proclaims the desirability of this
reticence.   "All that might be said on this topic," he observes, "is
not suitable to explain now or to all.   For the many need no
further teaching than the punishment of sinners.   For it is not
expedient to go further on account of those who scarcely through
the fear of eternal punishment restrain the outpouring into any
amount of reckle·sness."

The force of the remark is entirely answered in the text.   Christianity admits of no esoteric doctrines.   All the children of the
Church, be they ever so humble, have a right to all that any of her
teachers know.   It seems to us—to far more of us, and to far greater
and wiser men than is generally supposed—that the common teaching on the subject of Hell is *not true :* and the cause of God can
only be served by the utterance of truth.   "I have not written
unto you because ye know not the truth, but because ye know it,
and that no lie is of the truth."   1 John ii. 21.

The doctrine of "accommodation" (οἰκονομία, συγκατάβασις) was

and greatest of the Fathers did preach it, and many saints at whose feet I gladly sit have preached it in this age. And, if we see a truth, are we to be "liars for God"[1] by suppressing it, because those think it dangerous who believe in no more potent motive for virtue and the love of God than a ghastly terror? Are we to go before the very God of truth with a lie in our right hands? Richard Baxter—a saint of God if there ever was one—avowed his belief that even a suicide, if hurried by sudden passion into self-slaughter, may be saved, and "If," he nobly added, "if it should be objected that what I maintain may encourage suicide, I answer, I am not to tell a lie to prevent it!" We English can't do that. But, oh, my brethren, I am not afraid, I never shall be afraid, of doing harm by asking you "to think noble things of God." I am not afraid to bid you plead with Him

too prevalent with some of the Fathers, and there is good reason to think that it influenced St. Chrysostom on this very question.

[1] Job xiii. 7. "Will ye speak wickedly for God? and talk deceitfully for Him?"

in the spirit of righteous Abraham, " That be far
from Thee, Lord : shall not the Judge of all the earth
do right ?"[1]   I am not afraid to say of Him with
holy Paul, " Is there unrighteousness with God ?
God forbid !"[2] I am not afraid to plead with Him,
in that syllogism which, as Luther said, sums up
all the Psalms of David—" the God of pity pities
the wretched. We are wretched ; therefore "—not
surely in this short world only, but for ever—" God
will pity us."   Punish us ? Yes, punish us *because* He pities.   But " God judges that He may
teach, He never teaches that He may judge."
His æonian fire is the fire of love ; it is to purify,
not to torture ; it is to melt, and not to burn :—

> " We would be melted by the heat of love
>   By flames far fiercer than are blown to prove
>   And purge the silver ore adulterate."

God Himself tells us that " He afflicteth, not willingly, but for our profit, that we may be partakers

[1] Gen. xviii. 25.   [2] Rom. ix. 14.

of His holiness;" but could it be "for our profit" to be tortured for ever in a hopeless hell?
And shall He belie His own words? Our Church,
thank God—wiser than her wisest, tenderer than
her tenderest ministers—speaks not in such tones
in her burial service; and I, who believe in a God
whose name is Love—I, who rely with all my heart
on "the mercy of the Merciful," [1]—I who put my
whole trust and confidence in that living God who
is "the Saviour of all men"—I, who think that the
key to all the dreadful perplexities of life and
death lies in the belief that Christ lived and died
—I, for one, say, God forbid! I would rather go
to the instinct of the Christian saint than to the
system of the dogmatic theologian; I would
rather accept, as reflecting the mind of God, the
broad humanitarian charity, the keen and tender
sensibility of the Christian poet, than the hard

[1] The Sultan of Zanzibar when in England used the striking
expression, "Since my father was taken to the mercy of the
Merciful."

logic of the inflexible systematist.   And our
great living poet ends his dread "Vision of Sin"
in the very spirit of my text :—

> " At last I heard a voice upon the slope
> Cry to the summit, ' *Is there any hope?* '
> To which an answer pealed from that high land,
> But in a tongue no man could understand :
> And, on the glimmering summit far withdrawn,
> God made himself an awful rose of dawn."

2. Dismissing then all controversy, which I never
wish to introduce into this or into any pulpit,—
not thinking it well to answer that part of controversy which springs from mere ignorance or angry
prejudice, but realising, with deep responsibility,
the sacredness of this place, and desiring, in deep
humility, to lead aright the thoughts of men and
women of open minds and loving hearts,—I will
ask you to glance a little closer with me at God's
ways with man.   Not in idle speculation, not in the
interests of any dogma, but because, a few years
hence, death stares every one of us in the face, and
because the faith in the future may beneficently

H 2

influence our work in the present—let us, for a few moments, glance at what men are, and at what we may hope in the future for them and for ourselves.

3. There are, in the main, three classes of men : there are the saints; there are the reprobates; there is that vast intermediate class lying between yet shading off by infinite gradations from these two extremes.[1]

I. Of the saints, my brethren, I shall not speak ; their promise is sealed ; their lot is sure. Beautiful, holy souls, into whom, in all ages, entering, the Spirit of God hath made them friends of God and prophets,[2] these are the joy of heaven—they are the salt of earth. We, every one of us, are better for them, as the dull clods of the earth are better for the snowy hills whence the rivers flow ; as the stagnant air of earth is better for the pure winds which scatter the pestilence. Oh, what would the

---

[1] See the similar remark in the Talmud, *Rosh Hashanah*, f. 17, 1.
[2] Wisd. vii. 27.

world be—what would England be—what would
this huge oppressive city be—without them ? with
out the ten righteous, the thirty, the forty, the
fifty righteous, for whose sakes the heavens do
not burst to drown, with deluging rain,

> " The feeble vassals of lust, and anger, and wine,
>   The little hearts that know not how to forgive?"

What would this city be if it were nothing more
than one mad greedy coil of jarring slanders, of
reckless competition, of selfish luxury, of brutal
vice ?   Few, we know, are these saints of God,
and mostly poor, and often despised ; and yet
it is they alone who save the world from corruption by the gangrene of its vices, from dissolu-
tion by the centrifugal forces of its hate.   Their
gentle words break our fierce wranglings with the
balm of love ; their calm faces look in upon our
troubles with peace and hope :—

> " Ever their statues rise before us,
>   Our loftier brothers, but one in blood,
> At bed and table they lord it o'er us,
>   With looks of beauty and words of good."

A millionnaire, a successful man, though the world crawl at his feet, is but as the small 'dust of the balance; but, " O God, O God, give us saints!" About them we have no controversy. We know that they shall be happy; we know that God shall treasure them in the day when He maketh up His jewels ; we know that " eye hath not seen, nor ear heard, nor heart conceived " what God shall give to them that love Him.[1]

II. But if *they* be unassailably secure, eternally happy, what of the other extreme ? what of the reprobates ? We see sometimes an heroic virtue; would to God that we never saw also a brutal vice. Not far from here is a vast prison,[2] holding some 1,200 criminals.· Every time the great clock of Westminster booms out its chimes to the tune—

> " Lord, through this hour,
> Be Thou my guide ;
> So, by Thy power,
> No foot shall slide ; "

---

[1] 1 Cor. ii. 9.   [2] Millbank.

those prisoners hear it. Among them are some
who have got within the arm of the law, but are
hardly criminals at all; those might be even
liberated : others who have fallen into crime only
from surrounding temptations, and from natures
weak but not depraved ; these might be reclaimed :
but some there are whom those who know them
describe as filthy, cruel, brutal, irreclaimable, and
whom society gives up.[1] It is thus (but I have
been obliged altogether to soften down his words)
that a great living writer speaks of them : " Miserable distorted blockheads," he calls them, " with
faces as of dogs or oxen ; angry, sullen, degraded,
sons of greedy mutinous darkness ; base-natured
beings, on whom, in a maleficent, subterranean life
of London scoundrelism, the genius of darkness
has visibly set his seal. Who," he asks, " could
ever command these by love ? " A collar round

---

[1] Professor Tyndall quotes this remark from the conversation of a
governor of a prison ; and it is to be found in almost the same words
in a recent narrative of *Five Years' Penal Servitude.*

the neck, a cartwhip on the back, these, in an impartial and steady human hand, are what should be afforded them,—and he proposes, with all the speed possible, to make an end of them at once.[1] Well, my brethren, the punishment of crime is just, and society has a right by stern punishment to protect the innocent; yet I am glad that the Saviour of man spake never in terms like these. I rejoice that He rather said that He came to call sinners to repentance;[2] to seek and save the lost.[3] And if you ask me whether I must not believe in endless torments for these reprobates of earth, my answer is, Ay, for these and for thee, and for me too, unless we learn with all our hearts to love good and not evil; but whether God for Christ's sake may not enable us to do this even beyond the grave, if we have failed to do so in this life— I cannot say. I know that God hates sin, because He loves the soul which it destroys; I know that

---

[1] Carlyle, *Latter Day Pamphlets.*
[2] Matt. ix. 13.   [3] Matt. xviii. 11 ; Luke xv. 4, &c

"the path of that hatred is as the path of a
flaming sword; which he who hath eyes may see,
divinely beautiful and divinely terrible, everywhere burning, as with unquenchable fire, the
false and death-worthy from the true and life-
worthy." [1]   Yet I know also that for these Christ
died.   The bigot may judge their souls if he
likes; the Pharisee may consign them with con-
ventional orthodoxy to endless torment; but so
cannot and will not I.   " Forbear to judge," said the
holy king by the awful death-bed of Cardinal
Beaufort, who died and made no sign—

> " Forbear to judge, for we are sinners all !
> Close up his eyes, and draw the curtain close,
> And let us all to meditation." [2]

Born and bred as these have been, surrounded
as they have been from infancy with sights and
sounds of degradation, what should we have been,—
what wouldst thou have been, O comfortable bigot,

---

[1] Carlyle.   [2] *Henry VI.*, act iii. sc. 3.

or thou, O prosperous Pharisee—hadst thou had but
as small a chance as they? Pointing to a murderer
on his way to execution, " there," said a good and
holy man, " there, but for the grace of God, goes
John Bradford." If, as we look into the abyss of
our own hearts, we see infinite potentialities of
guilt and vice, so, as I look on these I see in
them, in spite of all their shame and stain, the infinite potentialities of virtue. And is it not almost
blasphemous to suppose that He who made a
human being with such rich capacities will in one
moment " throw it from Him into everlasting darkness ? " Not mine at any rate shall it be to close
against them " with impetuous recoil and jarring
sound," the gates of hell, lest those gates should
more justly be clanged on me ;[1] but I commend them
with humblest hope, even after this life of hope-
lessness, to Him who did not loathe the whiteness
of the leper, and who suffered the woman that

---

[1] James ii. 13. " He shall have judgment without mercy, that
showeth no mercy ; and mercy rejoiceth against judgment."

was a sinner to wash his feet with tears.[1]   That
without holiness none can see God; that every
guilty deed, if unrepented of, must bring its own
just and awful retribution; that, for every impure
and cruel soul there remaineth, behind the clouds
of this world, the dark night of the next; *that*
I know.   But when I remember that even these
have been known to burst into tears at a mother's
name; that even these have been known at times
to flash out into high deeds of momentary heroism—
I see that God's Spirit has nowhere taught us that
He who gave cannot give back; that He who once
made them innocent children cannot restore their
innocence again; that He who created them,—He
who will have all men to be saved,[2]—cannot re-
create them in His own image, cannot uncreate their
sins.   At any rate no arrogant word, no theologic
dogma, no acrid prejudice of mine, shall ever utter
to them the language of despair, or stand between
these—God's lowest—and His love.   Nay, I believe

---

[1] Luke xii. 48.   [2] 1 Tim. ii. 4.

that the Good Shepherd, for so He Himself has
told us, will not cease to search for these His
lost sheep, *until* He find them.[1]   Here again the
Christian poets teach us a truer charity than the
hard theologians :

> " Still for all slips of her,
>   One of Eve's family,
>   Wipe those poor lips of her,
>   Oozing so clammily.
>   *   *   *
>   Make no deep scrutiny
>   Into her mutiny. . .
>   Cross her hands humbly,
>   As if praying dumbly,
>   Over her breast.
>   *Owning her weakness,*
>   *Her evil behaviour,*
>   *And leaving with meekness*
>   *Her sin to her Saviour !"*

III. But, my brethren, the vast, vast mass of
mankind belong to the third class : they are not
utter reprobates any more than they are saints.
They may rise to the one, they may sink to the
other; but for the most part they are undecided.

---

[1] Luke xv. 4.

They face both ways; they halt between two
opinions; they are neither saints nor criminals;
they have *not* closed heart and soul with good, they
have not abandoned themselves utterly to evil.
They want to be pardoned, yet they want to
retain the offence; they admire holiness, but they
dally with iniquity; they shudder to be in a state
of sin, yet they attain not to a state of grace;
there "is an Adam in them, and there is a Christ;"[1]
now they sin with reckless abandonment, now they
repent in bitterest remorse; "the angel has them
by the hand and the serpent by the heart."[2]   To
how many here do these words apply?   We break
no law of man; to the eye of man it might seem
that we broke no law of God.   But O what
would be thought of us if we were all seen as
we are?—if our hearts were naked and open to
each other as they are to God?   And it is those
who do try to be God's children who most realise

---

[1] J. Martineau, *Endeavours after a Christian Life.*
[2] Ruskin.

their own exceeding sinfulness. This is why (as one has said) the cry of remorse and anguish which springs from the lips of a Fénélon or a Cowper is far more bitter than any confession which is ever wrung from a Richelieu or a Voltaire. Many, many of these better, and tenderer, and saintly souls have, I believe, been rendered utterly and hopelessly wretched, even to madness, as poor Cowper was, by that false view of God which is given by the pitiless anathemas of man. But to all these comes the cry, "*Comfort* ye, comfort ye, my people, saith our God."[1] Your own holier instinct tells you so. Son, or brother, or friend, or father dies : we all have lost them ; it may be that they were not holy ; not even religious ; perhaps not even moral men ; and it may be that, after living the common life of man, they died suddenly, and with no space for repentence ; and if a state of sin be not a state of grace, then certainly, by all rules of theology,

[1] Is. xl. 1.

they had not repented, they were not saved.
And yet, when you stood—O father, O brother—
heavy-hearted by their open grave;—when you
drank in the sweet words of calm and hope which
our Church utters over their poor remains;—
when you laid the white flowers on the coffin;—
when you heard the dull rattle of "earth to earth,
ashes to ashes, dust to dust;"—you,—who, if
you knew their sins and their failings, knew also
all that was good, and sweet, and amiable, and
true within them,—*dared* you, *did* you even in the
inmost sessions of thought,—consign them, as you
ought logically to do, as you ought if you are
sincere in that creed to do,—to the unending
anguish of that hell which you teach? Or does
your heart, your conscience, your sense of justice,
your love of Christ, your faith in God, your belief
in Him of whom you sing every Sunday that
His mercy is everlasting,—*rise* in *revolt* against
your nominal profession then? You *can* bear to
think of them,—as you can bear to think of your-

self—suffering, as they never did on earth, the
aching pang of God's revealing light, the willing
agony of His remedial fire. We should desire,—
we should even pray for that—the natural consequence of our own alienation—meant not to
torment us, but to perfect. But an arbitrary in-
fliction—a burning torment—an endless agony
—a material hell of worm and flame—a doom
to *everlasting sin ;* [1]—and all this with no prospect

---

[1] Mark iii. 29. "*All sins shall be forgiven unto the sons of men,
and blasphemies wherewithsoever they shall blaspheme :* but he that
shall blaspheme against the Holy Ghost hath never forgiveness, but
is in danger of *eternal sin* " (such is the true reading, ἁμαρτήματος,
א.B.L. ἁμαρτίας, C. D. *not* κρίσεως).

1. Now "hath never forgiveness," is οὐκ ἔχει ἄφεσιν εἰς τὸν αἰῶνα,
and it is superfluous to tell scholars that εἰς τὸν αἰῶνα no more
necessarily implies endlessness than לְעוֹלָם does. (See Excursus p. 197,
on αἰώνιος.)

2. Our Lord states with immense plainness, and with no reserva-
tion, the possible ultimate remission of every sin and blasphemy
except one.

3. What that one is no human being has ever been able to decide.

4. Even of that one it is only said (in the parallel passage, Matt.
xii. 32) that it shall not be remitted to him "either in this or in
the future age or ' dispensation' (αἰῶνι)."

I make no comments, but merely ask all men to weigh these passages.

of amendment, with no hope of relief—the soul's
transgressions of a few brief hours of struggling,
tempted life followed by billions of millenniums in
scorching fire—and all this meant, not to correct
but to harden; not to amend, but to torture and
degrade:—did you believe in *that* for those whom
you have loved? Again, I say, God forbid:—
again, I say, I fling from me with abhorrence such
a creed as that ! Let every Pharisee, if he will, be
angry with me—let every dogmatist anathematise
—but that I cannot, and do not believe. Scripture
will not let me ; my conscience, my reason, my faith
in Christ, the voice of the Spirit within my soul, will
not let me ; *God* will not let me! What I do
believe is this,—that for every wilful sin which we
commit, unless it be repented of, we shall, as we
do, feel the heavy and merciful wrath of God,
until He have purged the vile dross from us, and
made us as the fine gold for Himself. But what ?
Shall nature fill the hollows of her coarse rough
flints with purple amethyst ; shall she, out of

I

the grimy coal, over which the shivering beggar warms himself, form the diamond that trembles on the forehead of a queen; shall even man take the cast-off slag and worthless rubble of the furnace and educe from it his most glowing and lustrous dyes—and shall *God* not be able to make anything of His ruined souls? And what? shall *we* be able to pity and to love those that hate us; and to bless those who curse us; and to forgive those who have wronged us;—shall we be willing to pardon our prodigals and to call them home;— and shall God not be willing—(and if willing who shall dare to say that He is not able?)—beyond the grave? "Shall mortal man be more just than God? Shall man be more just than his Maker?" We made them not; they are not people of *our* pasture, or sheep of *our* hands; yet if we can feel for sinners a yearning love, a trembling pity; and if that love and pity springs from all that is holiest and most Christlike in our souls;—and if it would be wholly impossible for

any wretch among us to be so remorseless as to
doom his deadliest enemy to an endless vengeance,
—are we to believe this of God?—to believe that
He who planted mercy in us is merciless, and that
He will "hold us up with one hand and torment
us with the other," who knoweth our frame, and
remembereth that we are but dust? Or shall we
not rather believe, as the wise woman of Tekoah
said to David three thousand years ago, "We
must needs die, and are as water spilt on the
ground; and God does not take away life, but
devises devices that the wanderer may not for
ever be expelled from Him."[1] Yes, where sin
aboundeth grace shall much more abound.[2] If
God visits the sins of the fathers upon the
children unto the fourth generation of them
that hate Him,—He showeth mercy, not only
unto thousands, as our version has it, but "unto

---

[1] 2 Sam. xiv. 14 (see the commentaries on this passage).
[2] Rom. v. 20.

I 2

the thousandth and thousandth generation "[1] of them that love Him, and keep His commandments; and so always,—in God's promises, though not in man's systems,—in God's revelations though not in man's beliefs,—there is a vast overbalance of mercy above wrath. Ay, my brethren, fear not; have faith in God; think noble things of God; be sure that trust in the righteous God means the ultimate triumph of good over evil; —be sure that the cross of Christ, Christ's infinite atonement, Christ's plenteous redemption, means, —for all who do not utterly extinguish within their own souls the glimmering wick of love to God,[2]—the conversion of earth's sinners, far off it may be,— but *at last*, far off, at last,—into God's saints.

---

[1] Such is the true meaning of Ex. xx. 6, as the late Mr. Erskine of Linlathen was so fond of pointing out. The Hebrew is לַאֲלָפִים with which must be understood דּוֹרִים.

[2] In Matt. xxv. 8, the true rendering is, not "our lamps are *gone* out," but are *going* out—are being quenched (αἱ λαμπάδες ἡμῶν σβέννυνται).

" I say to thee, do thou repeat
    To the first man thou mayest meet
    In lane, highway, or open street,

" That he, and we, and all men move
    Under a canopy of love
    As broad as the blue sky above.

" And,—ere thou leave him,—say thou this,
    Yet one word more,—*they* only miss
    The winning of that final bliss,

" Who will not count it *true*, that love,
    Blessing, not cursing, rules above—
    And that in it we live and move.

" And one thing further make him know,
    That to believe these things are so,
    This firm faith never to forego,—

" *Despite* of all that seems at strife
    With blessing—all with curses rife—
    That *this is blessing—this is life !*"

(ARCHBISHOP TRENCH.)

SERMON V.[1]

EARTHLY AND FUTURE CONSEQUENCES OF SIN.

ROM. vi. 1.

"What shall we say then? Shall we continue in sin, that grace may abound? God forbid. How shall we, that are dead to sin, live any longer therein?"

WE are, my brethren, poor blind creatures at the best ; so one-sided, so imperfect, so liable to error, —so easily led astray by the pride which apes humility—so apt to be puffed up by the ignorance which takes itself for knowledge—that we constantly turn into banes what God intended as our richest boons, and store the very manna of His love in such earthen vessels of frailty and presumption, that, in our keeping, it breeds worms

[1] Preached in Westminster Abbey, Nov. 28, 1877.

and grows corrupt.   And hence even God's most
holy truths become liable to dreadful perversions.
It was so in the first ages when there were ungodly men who turned the grace of God into
lasciviousness.[1]   It was so again when Luther at
the Reformation shook down the hollow structure
of tradition which men had accepted as their
faith.   It may be so when we open to the despair
of the guilty even in the Valley of Achor a door
of hope, and ask men to take nobler and truer
views of God than those which run counter to
what the Scriptures teach us of His everlasting
mercy;[2] of His purpose in punishment being not
to torture but to redeem;[3] of the day when Christ
shall have triumphed for ever, and God shall be
all in all.[4]   I did not seek the topic, nor shall I
pursue it; but when it came in the ordinary
course of our meditations I could not but strive
to remove thoughts which, as I know, goad

---

[1] Jude 4.   [2] Ps. c. 5.   [3] Heb. xii 10.
[4] πάντα ἐν πᾶσι, "All things in all men."   1 Cor. xv. 28.

some men into wretchlessness and infidelity, and
embitter the hearts of others with a narrow,
railing, Pharisaic dogmatism, full of cursing bitterness against all who presume to differ from itself.
But there are deeper reasons than these for
preaching what we believe to be the truth on this
dim subject. The virtue which has no better
basis than fear of Hell is no virtue at all. No
virtue is in the least degree virtuous which springs
only from the hope of profit or the fear of
punishment. Although, for instance, honesty is
the best policy, yet, as was truly said by Archbishop Whately, " The man who is honest because it is the best policy is no better than a
rogue." Would you think much of one who only
did not commit murder because of the hangman?
or was only not a scoundrel from fear of being
found out? Fear may create the enforced obedi-
ence of the slave : love only can win the devotion
of the child ; and that is why God hath not sent
to us—who know the truth and whom the truth

has made free[1]—the spirit of fear and of bondage, but of love, and of power, and of a sound mind.[2] And this love is the sole eternal basis of holiness. To preach that God willeth all men to be saved —that is Gospel truth; to preach that it is not the love of Christ, but the fear of hell which con- straineth us—that is the soul-destroying error. What was the sum of the teaching of our Blessed Lord ?—was it "turn or burn"? or was it "Come unto Me, and I will give you rest"? Was it hell- fire that He preached to the rejoicing multitudes as He sat among the lilies above the silver lake? or was it the beatitudes of the meek and the merciful, and about a Father who maketh His sun to rise on the evil and on the good, and sendeth rain on the just and on the unjust? I know that He said with awful solemnity, "If thine eye offend thee, pluck it out; if thy hand offend thee, cut it off, and cast it from thee: it is better for thee to enter into life blind, or maimed, than, having two

[1] John viii. 32.   [2] 2 Tim. i. 7.

eyes or two hands, to go into Gehenna, into the
unquenchable fire, where their worm dieth not,
and the fire is not quenched." But what childish
vanity and arrogance is it to quote such texts
without knowing any of the laws of their meaning or their interpretation! It is just as childish
as it is to quote the words, " This is My body,"
and hold them to be decisive in proof of tran-
substantiation ; or to quote "them He did pre-
destinate" as decisive in proof of Calvinism. I
claim to speak with at least as much authority
as any one else when I say that there is not a
word here about that which neither the Roman
nor the Anglican Church requires us to believe
—viz., an irreversible doom at death, for all sinners,
to endless torments.[1] The language of our Blessed
Lord and Master is no more literal in the second
half of the verse than in the first. We have

---

[1] The *Catech. Trident.*, l. 6, *qu.* 3, uses language which seems to
imply endless torments *for some;* but I mainly allude to the
doctrine of Purgatory.

no more right to take the first half metaphorically and the second literally, than the youthful
Origen had to take the first half literally and
the second metaphorically. Our Lord speaks,
as He did habitually and designedly, in metaphors and parables; and His metaphors meant
this awful truth—that the most painful physical
agony and the worst physical mutilation is a
less anguish and a more trivial loss than that
shame and corruption which are the inevitable
consequence of sin—the flame of remorse which
will always burn so long as sin is practised; the
worm of conscience, which will always gnaw until
it is forgiven.[1]   Such a warning has no affinity with
that dogmatic and damnatory hatred which says,
" Hold this opinion or you will find yourself in a

[1] I have already spoken of the sole sense in which the Jews
understood the word Gehenna. The expression, " quenchless fire,"—
for the phrase "that *never shall be* quenched " is a simple mistranslation—is taken from Is. lxvi. 24, and is as purely a figure of speech,
as it is there, or as it is in Homer's *Iliad*, xvi. 123, and many other
passages.   The Gospel, like the law, speaks, as the Talmudic pro-
verb so wisely says, " in the tongue of the sons of men."

lake of inextinguishable fire." What our Saviour taught—what, thank God, we all agree in teaching, is this :—' Resist the evil which is in you, for it is your curse and ruin ; and until you have learnt to forsake and hate it, you cannot enter into the kingdom of heaven. Resist it because God hates it ; because God loves you ; because He desires to save you from it and from its deadly consequences. Resist it because it was to seek the lost that I came, and to redeem them that I died.' That is true, that is divine teaching.

> " So the All-Great is the All-Loving too,
> So through the thunder comes a human voice,
> Saying, ' O heart I made, a heart beats here ;
> Face my hands fashioned, see it in myself ;
> Thou hast no force, nor canst conceive of mine ;
> But love I gave thee, with myself to love,
> And thou must love me who have died for thee.' "

2. That then, my brethren, is the true motive for all holiness—Christ's redemption—God's love. We are dead with Christ unto sin ; we live to God unto righteousness.[1] And God created us, not to

[1] Rom. vi. 16.

destroy, not to torment, not to take vengeance on us, but to save, and to save us to the uttermost, from sin, from corruption, from that true Gehenna which is not a burning prison, but a polluted heart. Alienation from God; hatred of truth; hatred of purity; a hard, bitter, railing, loveless spirit; mean, base, selfish, sensual desires; these are the elements of hell:—and as long as any man,—be he Pharisee or be he publican,—is given to these, so long he will be made to feel with the evil spirit,

> " Which way I fly is hell, myself am hell,
> And in the lowest deep a lower deep,
> Still gaping to devour me, opens wide,
> To which the hell I suffer seems a heaven."

Hell is a temper, not a place. So long as we are evil, and impure, and unloving, so long where we are is hell, and where hell is there we must be; and when all the world dissolves, and every creature is purified, whom God's love *can* purify, then "all places shall be hell that are not heaven."[1]   How long, how far, we in our pride and obduracy and corruption may harden ourselves, even beyond the grave, against the constraining love of God, we know not, and none knows; but *so long as* we continue to do this, it is not God who is kindling for us His avenging tortures, but we who by our own impenitence are defeating His infinite purposes and destroying and ruining ourselves.   Good men, as I have said, may and do hold this doctrine of endless torture, with pity and fear and trembling, and awful submission; but let those men suspect their own hearts and their own purposes to whom so terrible a dogma—terrible even if it be true—is so dear,

---

[1] These lines from Marlowe's *Dr. Faustus*,

> " Hell hath no limits, nor is circumscribed
> In one self place : but where we are is hell,
> And where hell is there we must ever be.
> And, to be short, when all this world dissolves,
> And every creature shall be purified,
> All places shall be hell which are not heaven,"

bear a curious, though certainly accidental, resemblance to the views of Scotus Erigena (see p. 170), except that they do not so fully admit the ἀποκατάστασις πάντων.

and precious, and comforting, that they are quite
" distressed " at the thought of losing it, and never
seem so happy as when they are denouncing it on
others.   They bid me tremble ; but it is not I who
tremble.   When I stand before the bar of my
Maker, a humble and penitent sinner; when I
cry that my sins may be covered with the white
robe of my Saviour's merits, as the snow falls
upon a miry world ; when I admit before Him,
with shame and sorrow, that my very tears
want washing, and my repentance needs to be
repented of : yet not on *this* account shall I
fear.   Man may curse—Eliphaz the Temanite,
and Bildad the Shuhite, and Zophar the Naama-
thite, and all their company may protest—but
Thou, O Father, wilt not be angry with Thy child
because he thought—and tried to bid others think
just and noble things of thee : Thou, O Saviour,
wilt not frown at him because he trusted in the
infinitude of Thy compassion : and Thou, O Holy
Spirit, whose image is the soft stealing of the dew

and the golden hovering of the dove, wilt know that if he erred it was because he fixed his eyes, not on the glaring and baleful meteors of anathematising orthodoxy, but on the star of Bethlehem and the clouds that begin to shine about the coming of the Lord; and that—if perchance he erred—the light which led astray was light from heaven.

No! it is not I who tremble. Let the zeal of a damnatory religion tremble! Let those tremble who would turn the Gospel of salvation for most men into a threat of doom! Let those tremble who are indignant at the thoughts which see room for hope beyond the grave! If indeed they be in the right, still their tenet is one so harrowing that it should be uttered only as the true saints who believed it have uttered it, with tears, and trembling pity, and bated breath. But if there be one thing which He must loathe whose name is Love, it is the hallelujahs of exultant anathema, and the thinly-disguised hate which rages and protests with so fierce an ignorance against a trust in Mercy founded only on these two great doctrines (which they say they own)—the doctrine of Christ's infinite redemption; the doctrine of God's boundless love.[1]

3. But I have now said all that it seems my duty to say on this subject. I thank God from my heart that what I believe to be His truth, taught us by His own word, confirmed in us by His own Spirit, has proved a source of relief and comfort to thousands of hearts all over England; and I do not think it necessary to enter on the endless task of either repudiating misrepresentations or deigning to take notice of abuse. My object to-day is a wholly different one. It is to leave all those without excuse who, on the grounds of a

---

[1] I am alluding, not to humble and holy Christians who hold ' such opinions, but to men like the preacher described by Dr. Guthrie, who "declared that he had a bad opinion of the condition of those who did not rejoice that God's enemies were destroyed *without remedy*. I thought I saw the man stamping with his foot, and putting out the smoking flax. It was a horrible caricature of the Gospel."—*Life*, p. 511.

K

possible hope beyond the grave, try to make light
of sin.   And therefore, my brethren, and above all,
you who are young and ignorant, I earnestly ask
your whole attention while I rede you beware
how you wrest God's mercy to your own ruin.
Have any of you said, ‘Because we may never
cease to hope, therefore we may go on in
sin’? Ah, if you have said that, you must
indeed be in a gall of bitterness and a bond
of iniquity from which it is clear that no
horrible dread of an endless hell has saved you!
Dare any one, who professes and calls himself a Christian, say in his heart, “Let us continue in sin, that grace may abound”?[1]   Will
he—can he dare—to turn the grace of our God
into lasciviousness?[2] to count the blood of the
covenant wherewith he was sanctified an unholy
thing?[3] to say, ‘Because God loves me, therefore I will do that which He hates; because Christ
died for me, therefore—deliberately, unblushingly—

---

[1] Rom. vi. 1.   [2] Jude iv.   [3] Heb. x. 29

I will crucify Him afresh, and put Him to an open shame?[1] Because it is His long-suffering which calls me to repentance,[2] therefore He shall wait my time?' My brethren, there are two kinds of sin—wilful sin and willing sin. Wilful sin is that into which, because of the frailty of our nature, because of the strength of passion and temptation, — not loving, but loathing it — not seeking, but resisting it—not acquiescing in, but fighting and struggling against it,—we all some-times fall. This is the struggle in which God's Spirit striveth with our spirit, and out of which we humbly believe and hope that God will, at the last, grant unto us victory and for-giveness. But there is another kind of sin,— far deadlier, far more heinous, far more incurable, —it is *willing* sin. It is when we are content with sin ; when we have sold ourselves to sin ; when we no longer fight against sin ; when we mean to continue in sin. That is the darkest, lowest,

[1] Heb. vi. 6.   [2] 1 Pet. iii. 20.

K 2

deadliest, most irredeemable abysm of sin ; and it is well that the foolish or guilty soul should know that on it, if it have sunk to this, has been already executed,—self-executed—the dread mandate, " In the day that thou eatest thereof, thou shalt surely die." [1]   By that curse was not meant a physical, but a spiritual death. The man who is sold under sin is dead,—morally dead, spiritually dead ;—and such a man is a ghost, far more awful than the soul which was once in a dead body, for he is a body bearing about with him a dead soul.   Better, far, far better for him to have cut off the right hand, or plucked out the right eye, than to have been cast as he has been, now in his lifetime—and as he will be cast until he repent, even beyond the grave—into that Gehenna of æonian fire! It shall purify him, God

---

[1] It is astonishing that this text should be quoted as though it had the very slightest bearing on this subject. In what sense is any one more guilty of preaching the devil's falsehood " Ye shall not die," by urging that there may be a hope *beyond* the grave, than we all are by urging that there is a hope on this side the grave ? Neither logic, nor charity, nor common sense have any share in such arguments.

grant, in due time; but oh! it shall agonise, because he has made himself, as yet, incapable of any other redemption. So that if any youth have wickedly thought in his heart that God is even such an one as himself—that he may break with impunity God's awful commandments, that he may indulge with impunity his own evil lusts, let him recall the sad experience of Solomon, which he heard this morning, " Walk in the ways of thine heart and in the sight of thine eyes : but know thou, that for all these things God will bring thee into judgment ; "[1] let him remember the stern warning of Isaiah, " Woe unto them that call evil good and good evil ; that put darkness for light, and light for darkness ; that put bitter for sweet, and sweet for bitter! Therefore as the fire devoureth the stubble, and the flame consumeth the chaff, so their root shall be as rottenness, and their blossom shall go up as dust: because they have cast away the law of the Lord of Hosts,

[1] Eccl. xi. 9.

and despised the word of the Holy One of Israel." [1]

I. For first, my brethren, let us all learn that the consequences of sin are *inevitable;* in other words, that punishment is but 'the stream of consequence flowing on unchecked.' There is in human nature an element of the gambler, willing to take the chances of things ; willing to run a risk if the issue be uncertain. There is no such element here. The punishment of sin is certain. All Scripture tells us so. "The soul that sinneth, it shall die."[2] "Be sure your sin will find you out."[3] "Though hand join in hand, the wicked shall not be unpunished."[4] "The way of transgressors is hard."[5]

All the world's proverbs tell us so. "Reckless youth, rueful age." "As he has made his bed, so he must lie in it." "He who will not be ruled by the rudder, must be ruled by the rock."

[1] Is. v. 24.   [2] Ezek. xviii. 4.   [3] Numb. xxxii. 23.
[4] Prov. xi. 21.   [5] Prov. xiii. 15.

Even Satan himself would not deny it. In the old legend of Dr. Faustus, when he bids the devil lay aside his devilish propensity to lying, and tell the truth, the devil answers, " The world does me injustice to tax me with lies. Let me ask their conscience if I have ever deceived them into believing that a bad action was a good one."

Even bad men admit it. They would gladly preach, if they could, that sin is but "a soft infirmity in the blood, not to be too severely visited ;" but the facts are too fatally against them, and those facts say, with unglosing voice, " If any man defile the temple of God, him shall God destroy."[1]

So that you see, on the testimony alike of the deceived and the deceiver, the punishment of sin is (first)—inevitable.

II. Notice, too, secondly, that the punishment of sin is *impartial*. There is a form of self-deception common to all of us, and especially in youth, by

---

[1] 1 Cor. iii. 17.

which we admit the general law, but try to shirk
its personal, individual application.   It is the old,
old story of Eden over again, in the case of every
one of us ; the serpent, creeping up to us all
glitter and fascination, all dulcet flattery and
sinuous glide, and whispering, ' See the fruit how
fair it is ; how much to be desired ; be as a god
knowing good and evil ; thou shalt not surely die ; '
and so the boy and the youth, healthy, and bright,
and gay, and even, in his folly, the grown man,
believes that it shall not be so with *him ;* that he
will repent in time ; that he is the darling of Providence, *he* the favourite of Heaven, *he* the one who
may sin and shall not suffer.   If others handle
pitch they shall be defiled ; if others take fire into
their bosom, they shall be burned ;[1] but God will
indulge *him ;* and the very spirits of evil laugh at
each one going as an ox to the slaughter, whom
they dupe into the fancy that out of special favour
to him " this adamantine chain of moral gravita-

[1] Prov. vi. 27.

tion, more lasting and binding than that by which the stars are held in their spheres, will be snapped ; that sin for him will change its nature,"[1] and at his approach the Gehenna of punishment be transformed into a garden of delight. Is it so ? Has there been any human being yet, since time began, however noble, however beautiful, however gifted, however bright with genius or radiant with fascination, who has sinned with impunity ? Ah, no ! God is no respecter of persons. Fire burns and water drowns, whether the sufferer be a worthless villain, or a fair and gentle child ; and so the moral law works, whether the sinner be a " David or a Judas, whether he be publican or priest." In the physical world there is no forgiveness of sins. Sin and punishment, as Plato said, walk this world with their heads tied together ; and the rivet that links their iron link is a rivet of adamant. 'A man who cannot swim might as well walk into a river,

[1] Archd. Hare.

and hope it will not drown, as a man, seeing judgment and not mercy denounced on willing sin,
hope that it will turn out to be mercy and not
judgment, and so defy God's law.'[1]   Will he
escape? O boy, O man, wilt thou escape? Ah
no! if you choose sin you will meet with retribution; and experience, in your own person, the *lex
talionis* of offended nature,—"eye for eye, tooth
for tooth, hand for hand, burning for burning, wound
for wound, stripe for stripe."[2]

III. You see then that the punishment of sin is
inevitable, and is impartial, and now see *why* it is
so.   It is so because the punishment of sin is not
an arbitrary interference, but a necessary *law*.   I
do not mean that God never directly interferes.
He does.   We see it daily in the history of crime.
We see it in strange detections; in providential
accidents; in the infatuations of penal stupidity
shown by able men bent on concealed wickedness.

[1] Irving.   [2] Ex. xxi. 24.

But leaving out of account these obvious visitations in which

> " God's terrible and fiery finger
> Shrivels the falsehood from the souls of men,"

there is generally a frightful resemblance which shows that the penalty is a genuine child of the transgression. We receive the things that we have done. There is a dreadful coercion in our own iniquities ; an inevitable congruity between the deed and its consequences ; an awful germ of identity in the seed and in the fruit. We recognise the sown wind in the harvest whirlwind.[1] We feel that it is we who have winged the very arrows that eat into our heart like fire. It needs no gathered lightning, no divine intervention, no miraculous message, to avenge in us God's violated laws. They avenge themselves. You may laugh at Bibles, sneer at clergymen, keep away from churches, and yet your sin, coming after you with leaden footstep, and gathering form, and towering over you, smites you

[1] Hos. viii. 7.

at last with the iron hand of its own revenge. I
cannot pretend to work out now the whole vast
scheme of this sacred Nemesis, or read for you, on
the wall of guilty hearts, this Mene, Mene, Tekel,
Peres of reddening doom. It would need a picture
such as when

> " Some great painter dips
> His pencil in the hues of earthquake and eclipse "—

it would need a voice like that which he who saw
the Apocalypse heard cry in the heaven aloud—
"Woe to the inhabiters of earth." But—for no
one shall say that he went unwarned; no one
shall shield himself under the plea that sin was
robbed, for him, of one true element of awfulness,
—I will tell you of one or two ways in which, if
God's love avail not, His terrors may at least
leave us in no doubt as to what He hates. Sleep
under it you who will, but if your souls be really
in earnest in inquiring about this matter I will
try for a few moments to accentuate for you some
syllables of that Voice behind thee saying, " This

is the way, walk ye in it," when ye turn aside to the right hand or to the left.

IV. Well, then, take *disease* as one form of the working of this inevitable law. Not always of course the direct result of sin, yet how much of it is directly due to dirt, neglect, folly, ignorance, the infected blood, the inherited instincts of this sad world? But are there not some diseases, and those of the most terrible which earth knows, which do spring directly, immediately, exclusively, undeniably from violations of God's law? Is not madness, very often, such a disease? Is there not, at this moment, many a miserable, degraded lunatic, who never would have been such but for repeated transgressions of God's known will?

Is there not again in the very life-blood of millions an hereditary taint,—blighting their health— poisoning as with a fury's breath the flower of their happiness — breaking out afresh in new generations — which has its sole source and origin in uncleanness?

Is there not, too, an executioner of justice told off to wait upon drunkenness—which would cease to exist if drunkenness ceased to exist ;—which is God's warning against that fearful intemperance against which senates will not fight, and they who love their fellows fight as yet in vain? Have you ever seen—if not, may you never see!—a young man suffering from delirium tremens? Have you heard him describe its horrors,—horrors such as not even Dante imagined in the most harrowing scenes of his *Inferno*—" the blood-red suffusion before the eyes quenched suddenly in darkness—the myriads of burning, whirling rings of concentric fire—millions of foul insects seeming to weave their damp, soft webs about the face—the bloated, hideous, ever-changing faces of their visions—the eyes that glare from wall to roof—the feeling as if a man were falling, falling, falling, falling, endlessly, into a fathomless abyss." *Why* is all this? Because *God* inflicts it on man? No, but because man inflicts it on himself ; and the God who loves us, wishing us to see how drunkenness blasts, and scathes, and debases, and imbrutes,—to save men from all this horrible stain, and agony, and shame, has attached this law to the abuse of intoxicating drinks, exactly as, to save us from handling fire, He causes fire to burn. Does God interfere ? No, but He says, O my son whom I have made,—this is the signboard of thy tippling-house,—this is the goal to which Intemperance leads ; as thou lovest Me, as thou lovest thine own soul, cut off thy right hand, pluck out thy right eye; it is better for thee to enter into life blind or maimed rather than cast thyself into this Gehenna of æonian fire—this depth of disgrace and of corruption—where the worm of the drunkard dieth not, and his fire is not quenched.

V. Or take any one, not of the physical, but of the moral workings of this law of punishment. Read with me *another* syllable of this handwriting upon the wall. Take *Fear* for instance. You

have heard of haunted houses : have you ever
heard of haunted men ? Are there any here who
are groaning under the burden of undetected sin ?
If so will they not recognise themselves as suffering this Nemesis of fear ? As there are some men
whose sins are open, going before to judgment—
marshalling them in undisguised array to the very
judgment-seat—so there are some men whose sins
follow after. There are men everywhere—there
are probably men here now—who ever, as they
walk through life, hear footsteps behind them ;
for whom "the earth is made of glass,"—on whom
the stars seem to look down as spies ; men whose
pulses shake at every sudden ring of the door-
bell—whose faces blanch if they be suddenly
accosted—who tremble if a steady gaze be fixed
upon them. Have not such men,—abject in the
dismay and weakness to which sin has reduced
them—thousands of times betrayed themselves
by their own unreasonable fears, and by imagining
that *their* sin was being spoken of, when some-

thing quite different was being spoken of? I
think it is the ancient writer Plutarch, in his remarkable pamphlet " On the Delayed Vengeance of
Deity," who tells how a youth, on being reproached
for his cruelty in fiercely wringing the necks of
some young birds, betrayed his hideous crime by
exclaiming, " It was their own fault : why did they
keep twittering at me ' Parricide, Parricide!'"
Take the life even of David.   After he had sent
that fatal letter to Joab about Uriah, do you think
that he ever had a moment's peace afterwards ?
Was not his own servant his master new, because
he knew his guilty secret ?   And if there be one
here who has done deeds which he would give
worlds to have left undone ;—about whose roof
is heard 'the flapping of unclean wings' ;—who
never again, in this world, shall sleep the sleep of
the innocent ;—for whom the "furies have taken
their seats upon the midnight pillow,"—on whose
breast, through the dark hours, ill dreams ride
heavily in the shape of his deadliest sin ;—will such

L

as these tell you that they were lucky not to have been caught?—happy in that they were not found out?—fortunate in that no stroke of detection or punishment arrested them before fruition, and in mid career?—

Achan concealed his theft; never spent his wedge of gold; never wore his Babylonish garment; yet, when discovery crept nearer and nearer to him, and at last touched him; when the lot fell and the tribe of Judah was taken; and the lot fell again, and the family of the Zarhites was taken; and the lot fell again, and the household of Zabdi was taken; and the lot fell once more, and Achan, the son of Carmi, the son of Zabdi, the son of Zerah, of the tribe of Judah, was taken, and was stoned, and burned, he, and his family, with the accursed, stolen thing, in the valley of Achor, did not Joshua indicate to him that detection might be a *blessed* thing? Did not he too, as I have done, open in the valley of Achor a door of hope, when he said to the exposed criminal, " My son, give, I pray thee, glory to the Lord God of Israel ; and tell me now what thou hast done ; hide it not from me " ? And would not Achan too have cause to say,

> " Minds which verily repent
> Are burdened with impunity
> And comforted by chast isement :
> That punishment's the best to bear
> That follows soonest on the sin,
> And guilt's a game where losers fare
> Better than those who seem to win." [1]

VI. But you will say, " There are many sins whose commission involves no great fear." Yes, truly ; but if the soul have any life left in it, when one ray of God's eternity shines into it, shame and the agonising sense of lost worth and self-loathing comes withal. When our first parents had tasted the fruit, then their eyes were miserably opened.

> " Innocence, that as a veil
> Had shadowed them from knowing ill, was gone,
> Just confidence, and native righteousness,
> And honour from about them, naked, left
> To guilty shame." [2]

---

[1] Coventry Patmore.   [2] Milton, *Paradise Lost*.

Ah, my brethren, have none of you, even very early, felt the working of this law? Have you known but for one hour what it is to be utterly miserably, intolerably ashamed of yourself? If so, you, too, have been in that Gehenna of æonian fire of which your Saviour speaks. It is the glare of illumination which the conscience flings over the soul after a deed of darkness. It is the revulsion of feeling on which we did not calculate when we have done with the sin, but the sin has not done with us. It is the little grain of conscience, within the very worst of us, which makes forbidden pleasures sour. It is the fact that none of us can be quite wicked enough really to enjoy wickedness. It is the aching crave after the brief intoxication. It is the Dead Sea apple shrivelling into hideousness the moment it has been tasted. It is the horror of the murderer when his passion of revenge is spent, and the cold grey dawn reveals the face of his murdered victim. It is the waking of the famished wretch who

has dreamt of food and water, and he wakes, and
lo! he is sick of hunger and scorched with thirst.
It is the cry from ten thousand biographies of
those who have sinned and suffered :—

> " When I received this volume small
> My years were barely seventeen,
> When it was hoped I should be all
> Which once, alas ! I might have been.

> " And now my years are thirty-five;
> And every mother hopes her lamb,
> And every happy child alive,
> May *never* be what I now am !" [1]

So, my brethren, you see, the very youngest of
you, that, if you choose sin you must have sin
as your *companion;* sin in her own hideous
presence, and with her the *death* which ever dogs
her footstep, and notches against her his arrow
on the string. I am not even pretending to show
you all the workings of that inevitable, impartial
law which we, in our loneliness and alienation, call

---

[1] Lines written by Hartley Coleridge in his Bible.

the heavy wrath of God. It is but as if I plucked one leaf and showed it you as a specimen of the boundless forest; it is but as if I showed you one little wave, and told you that a whole ocean was behind. But I will only ask you to glance at one more feature of this law. There shall be (let us suppose it) no intervention; no sickness; no detection; no shame even; no fear; no outward and visible punishment of any kind. Conscience shall, for a time, be dead; life shall, for years, be prosperous. Does sin escape then? Is the sinner happy then? Ah no! he is worst off then. *"Nulla pœna, quanta pœna!"*[1] This is God's worst, severest punishment. "Ephraim is joined to idols!" What then? Arrest him as with the punishment of a dear and pleasant child? Make him sick with smiting him into penitence? Ah, no! worse than that—*let him alone;*[2] blind his eyes; put the scourge in his own hand; let him strut to his confusion; let the guilt which he has chosen come into his bowels

---

[1] Augustine.   [2] Hos. iv. 17.

like water and like oil into his bones ; let *sin* be the deadliest executioner, the most merciless avenger of sin. Let the acute pang become the chronic malady. Let the thought become the wish, and the wish the act, and the act the habit. Let the solitary become the frequent, the frequent the incessant, the incessant the all-but-necessary, all-but-inevitable transgression. Let *crime* awake him. Let the serpent's egg become a cockatrice, and its seed a fiery flying serpent. Let hatred become murder; let ambition become conspiracy ; let greed become theft and swindling : let lust become some deadly impurity. Ah ! when God sends forth a besetting sin—a guilty habit—to be His executioner, the case is most awful, most hopeless then. God only, by Christ's redemption, can save from the body of that death !

My brethren, will you now say that " I will go on in sin, and it does not matter ?" Ah ! but, most terribly and awfully, it does matter ! You may be saved indeed, at last, if God will ; saved, not from

Him and His wrath, but from yourself and your
own self-destruction ; but even then there is a
sense in which it may be awfully true that our
millenniums depend upon our moments; and
though God's infinite love may be able to save you,
yet, alas! it may only be as a brand is plucked,
half-consumed, out of the burning ; "as a shepherd
tears out of the mouth of a lion two legs and the
piece of an ear!"[1]   Do not think that repentance
is an easy thing, and be quite sure of this, that the
longer it is delayed the less easy does it become,
and the more terrible are the consequences—both
here and hereafter—which the delay involves.

> " A spotless child sleeps on the flowering moss :
>   'Tis well for him ; but if a guilty man,
>   Envying such slumber, should desire to put
>   His guilt away, can he return to rest
>   At once by lying there ?   Our sires knew well
>   The fitting course for such : dark cells, dim lamps,
>   A stone floor one may writhe on like a worm,
>   No mossy pillow blue with violets."[2]

---

[1] Amos. iii. 12.   [2] Browning's *Paracelsus.*

The path of *repentance* may never be closed to
us; so I believe the Catholic Church of Christ
has in most ages taught; but O how hard may that
path of repentance be! over what bleeding flints;
through what a scorch of fiery swords; through
what deep shame, what dread corruption, what
pain of body, what misery of remorse, what agony
of soul! O! were it not better to cut off the right
hand, and pluck out the right eye, than go of our
own choice into the Gehenna of æonian fire, here
and hereafter, such as I believe that Christ meant,
and such as I have now in part only—in shadow
and in outline—described?   God is the Lord
God, merciful and gracious, long-suffering and
of great mercy, forgiving iniquity and transgression and sin,—and yet by no means clearing the
guilty. Why? Because He loves us not? Not
so, for "God's severity is all love"; but because
sin is the one deadly enemy which He must
destroy in us, lest it destroy us, and we, with it,

destroy ourselves; He must destroy it for our sakes, because, as you will hear just now in glorious music,

> " The greatness of His mercy reacheth unto the heavens,
> And His truth unto the clouds."

BRIEF SKETCH OF ESCHATOLOGICAL OPINIONS IN THE CHURCH.

THE Scriptures reveal indeed a future state of retribution, but are—when competently interpreted in the light of modern criticism—absolutely silent as to "endless torture"; or, if this be not conceded, they at least seem to express with the utmost possible plainness a view of Final Restitution which cannot be reconciled with the ultimate and all-but-universal perpetuity of sin. Hence the language of the Fathers, who freely adopted both sets of phrases, is frequently self-contradictory. In the earliest of them—Justin Martyr and Irenæus—are some well-known passages which seem clearly to imply either the ultimate redemption or the total destruction of sinners; and though

they also use language which may be interpreted in accordance with a belief in endless
torments, it is by no means clear that the phrases
they adopt may not be meant in the same sense in
which we believe them also to be used in Scripture.

It was in answer to the bitter taunt of Celsus,
that the God of the Christians kindled a fire in
which all except Christians should be burned, that
Origen first argued that the fire should possess
a purifying quality (καθάρσιον) for all those who
had in themselves any materials for it to consume ;
any wood, hay, stubble in their thoughts and theological systems. All, he said, even Peter and Paul,
must pass through this fire (Is. xliii. 2), and ordinary sinners must remain in it till purged. It is in
fact a baptism of fire, at the second resurrection,
for those who had not received effectually the
baptism of the Spirit (Περὶ ἀρχῶν, i. 6, C. Cels. vi. 26 ;
Hom. in Psalm iii. 1; in Jerem. ii. 3; in Ezek. i. 13).
It was not a material fire, but self-kindled, like
an internal fever. It was in fact remorse for

remembered sin, a "figurative representation of the moral process by which restoration shall be effected." The English Church, which condemned in Article 22 the "Romish" doctrine of Purgatory, never condemned these merciful opinions, which have always been more or less prevalent in the Greek Church.

Clemens of Alexandria (*Strom.* vii. 6) had already spoken of the fire as a sort of spiritual fire (πῦρ φρόνιμον), which does not burn the flesh, but purifies the soul. And though he does not express himself with perfect distinctness, yet the whole drift of his remarks proves that he could not have held an unmitigated doctrine of endless punishment, but only of a punishment which would necessarily cease when its remedial object was attained (see Baur, *Dogmengeschichte*, i. 718). And Clemens, like Origen, seems to imply an ultimate amendment of every evil nature (*Strom.* i. 17, § 86 ; vii. 2 ; *Pædag.* i. 8—10) in something of the same spirit as the modern poet—

" O wad ye tak a thocht and men',
　Ye aiblins might, I dinna ken,
　　Still hae a stake ;
　I'm loath to think upon yon den
　　E'en for your sake."[1]

Satan, in the opinion of Origen, is " the last
enemy ; " but his " destruction " means that he
ceases to be an enemy. God, he says, made no
being irreclaimable, but all for a good purpose,
and creatures thus produced cannot be annihilated.
The final reconciliation will be universal. (On this
esoteric doctrine of restitution see Orig. *De Princip.*

---

[1] It is, I think, demonstrable that this opinion of the salva-
bility of devils (a question which I set aside as beyond our range)
gave far deeper offence than the peculiar universalism of Origen as
regards mankind (see Jer. *adv. Pelag.* i. 9). For the views of Clemens
on the purifying intelligential fire, see *Strom.* vii. 6, *ad fin. ;* on the
hope beyond the grave (ἐπεὶ μηδεὶς τόπος ἀργὸς εὐποιΐας Θεοῦ), *id.*
iv. 6, § 37 ; vi. f. 638, 639 ; on the intention of punishment as a
benefit (πρὸς τὸ χρήσιμον) both collectively and individually to those
who are punished, *Pædag.* i. 8, *passim, Strom.* vii. 13, 14, 16, and
a striking passage in the *Fragm. in* 1 *Joh.* (ed. Pott, p. 1009, cf.
Theodoret *In Ezech.* vi. 6) ; on Christ's preaching to the dead, see
Strom. vi. 6 (cf. Hermas. iii. 16). The remedial fire of the Alexandrians, &c. (πῦρ φρόνιμον, καθάρσιον, σωφρονοῦν) differs from
purgatory, because it is (i.) *after* the resurrection, and (ii.) not *instead
of* Hell (Bishop Harold Browne, *Articles,* pp. 498—450).

iii. 6, 6; i. 6. 3; ii. 8, §§ 4—8; *c. Cels.* vi. 26; Neander, ii. 437; Hagenbach, i. 242.) That these particular views have never been condemned by any decree of the Universal Church is certain. Neither the Fifth nor any other Œcumenical Council, nor even the " Home Synod " of A.D. 541, ever condemned the tenet of a hope for the lost even beyond the grave. (See Cave, *Hist. Liter.*, p. 548; Hefele, *Concilien-Geschichte*, ii. 759—764; Dean Stanley, *Essay on Church and State*, pp. 137, 318; F. N. Oxenham, *Letter on Everlasting Punishment*, pp. 17—25.)

The views of Gregory of Nyssa were (*Or. cat.* viii.; and xxxv. and Περὶ Ψυχῆς, *Opp.* ii. 12; iii. 226—229, &c.: ed. Paris, 1630), that the soul, having an affinity to God, must ultimately return to God; and that the anguish it must suffer is necessarily caused during the separation of good from evil, not from any desire on God's part to torment. Hence all evil will ultimately disappear. Virtue is in this life the purification of the soul, and

if during life it has not been cured from vice, it
may be purified hereafter by the baptism of fire,
and all things will at last serve God. All punishment is educational, purgatorial, remedial in its
object.[1] The writings of this great Father are
most important as proving the permissibility of
these views. His authority stood deservedly high
as a great and persecuted champion of the Nicene
faith, and his orthodoxy was so unimpeachable
that he was one of the most prominent figures
at the Council of Constantinople, "his advice
being chiefly relied upon in the most important cases ; and therefore when it was thought
necessary to make an explanatory confession of
faith, especially in the Article of the Holy Ghost,
the drawing it up was committed to his care,
and this is the Constantinopolitan, or, as among
us it is called, the Nicene Creed."

---

[1] Cave, *Lives of the Primitive Fathers*, ii. *ad fin.* See Niceph.
Coll. xiii. 13. Even if Gregory did not (as Nicephorus asserts) draw
up the changes and additions of the Nicene Creed, yet he occupied a
most commanding position at the Council of Constantinople (Möhler

The traces of the same doctrine in Diodorus of Tarsus, Didymus of Alexandria, and Gregory of Nazianzus are slight, but φωνᾶντα συνετοῖσιν. When the latter speaks of one kind of fire as being annihilative, but adds, "unless it be more humane

in Herzog, *Encycl. s. v.*, quoting *Cod. Theod.* i. 63, Sozomen II.E. vii. 6, Socrates H.E. v. 8, and Gregory, *Opp.* iii. 645). It is true that these additions occur in a work of Epiphanius several years before the First Council of Constantinople (De Broglie, *L'Église et l'Empire Romain*, v. 451), but Gregory's authority must have aided their acceptance, and therefore it must have been more than per-missible to accept the clauses about a future life in the sense which he attached to them—a sense such as to include "the blessed hope that God's justice and mercy are not controlled by the powers of evil, that sin is not everlasting, and that in the world to come punish-ment will be corrective and not final, and will be ordered by a love and justice, the height and depths of which we cannot here fathom or comprehend" (Dean Stanley, *Essays on Church and State*, 318, &c.). No scholar will now revive the attempts of Germanus in the eighth century, and of Tillemont (*Mém.* ix. 561, *sqq.*) to regard as interpolations such passages as those to which I have referred. Vincenzo in his work quotes other passages of a different apparent tendency, but this is due to the varying character of the Scriptural evidence. Let those, at least, who in sheer ignorance impugn the Gospel of Eternal Hope, remember that it was openly preached by this canonised Saint and Bishop—the "Father of Fathers"—whose writings were referred to by the Council of Ephesus as the great bulwark of the Church against heresy !

M

to perceive even here the action of beneficence, and worthily of Him who punishes " (φιλανθρωπότερον καὶ τοῦ κολάζοντος ἐπαξίως), it is clear that the great Patriarch of Constantinople—he who earned the title of " The Theologian "—leaves this an open question. (*Or.* xxxix. 19 ; xl. 36 ; xxx. 6, &c.)

Even teachers who were in other respects opposed to Origen adopted this view, namely, Diodorus of Tarsus in his Περὶ Οἰκονομίας, and Theodore of Mopsuetia in his commentary on the Gospels. They grounded their objections to the popular doctrine upon the disproportionateness of endless punishment to the sins of a brief life ; upon the mercy of God ; and upon the impossibility of imagining that the wicked would be purposelessly raised from the dead only to be tormented, without any capacity for amendment.[1]

---

[1] The views of these great teachers may be found, as quoted by a Nestorian bishop, in Assemanni, *Bibliotheca Orientalis*, iii. 323 *seqq.*, Photius, *Bibl. Cod.* 81. On the prevalence of this opinion both in the East and West see Neander, iv. 456, E. Tr. Hagenbach. i. 245 ; Haag, *Hist. des Dogmes*, ii. 342 ; Gieseler, i. 362, E. Tr.

These opinions were indeed rejected by individual theologians, but (as I have pointed out in Sermon III., p. 85) in a tone which, because it springs from deeper knowledge, is far more sympathetic, and far more respectful, than that adopted by the most ignorant of modern controversialists.

Thus, St. Athanasius—who might have been supposed to have as keen an eye for heresy as any one—so far from speaking angrily of Origen—Origen the adamantine—Origen the holy, the self-denying, the pre-eminently learned—whom it is the fashion to place below St. Augustine, but who in every respect, except a power of rhetoric, was his superior—speaks of him tenderly and admiringly as "the marvellous and indefatigable Origen" (ὁ θαυμαστὸς καὶ φιλοπονώτατος),[1] and in one passage only alludes with oblique and kindly disapproval to his opinion on the Restitution of all things.[2]

---

[1] *De Com. essent.* tom. i. p. 236.

[2] Cave, *Lives of the Primitive Fathers*, i. 23.

M 2

St. Ambrose, though using the ordinary phraseology in some places, distinctly states the doctrine of universal restitution (*Comment. in Ps.* xxxv. 15, cxix. 153; *cf.* Ambrosiaster in *Ep. ad Eph.* ii. iii.).

St. Augustine admits that not only some, but very many (*nonnulli immo quam plurimi*) held this merciful view; and although he devotes the twenty-first book of his *De Civitate Dei* to what he supposes to be a refutation of their opinion— a refutation which however turns out, on examination, to be nothing remotely resembling a refutation, and to be indeed little more than an assertion of his own interpretations of various texts —calls them "our party of pity" (*nostri misericordes*), and deals with them in perfect courtesy and toleration (*pacificè disputandum*). Moreover, it is in the *De Doctrinâ Christianâ* of St. Augustine that we find the first distinct outline of that doctrine of Purgatory which robs the opinion of endless torments of its most pressing horrors,

(See *De Civ. Dei*, xx. 25, &c. ; Cyrill. *Catech.* 15, § 9; Orig. *C. Cels.* v. 15, &c.)   The tone adopted by St. Augustine proves that he is dealing with a matter not of faith, but of opinion ; and without sanctioning, he yet did not reject the belief that even amid endless punishment God might show His mercy by various alleviations. His view is therefore far less dark and intolerable than that of post-Reformation theologians (*De Civ. Dei*, xx. ; *Enchir.* 29, &c.) ; and it is absolutely indisputable that both the opinions of St. Augustine, and those of the Fathers in general, approximate far more nearly to those which I have here advocated than the more modern and popular theory of current teaching.

St. Jerome, fiercely as he opposed Origenists, yet held Origen's opinions on future Restoration, so far at any rate as Christians are concerned. In his letter to Avitus he treats the question as an open one, and holds "Christianos, *si in peccatis praeventi fuerint*, salvandos esse post poenas."

(See *Adv. Pelag.* i. 9; *Adv. Rufin.* ii. 1; in Jes. *ad fin;* in Eph. iv. § 12; Gal. v. 22, &c.) If it be averred that the opinion "*supplicia aliquando finiri et post multa tempora terminum habere tormenta,*"—which St. Jerome tells us was common in his day,— merely implied the end of pain (*poena sensûs*) not the end of loss (damnation, *poena damni*), it is still clear that the views of the early Church were far . less ruthless than those of the present day.

As to Councils, "none of the first four General Councils lay down any doctrine whatever concerning the everlasting misery of the wicked, or directly or indirectly give any interpretation of the Scriptural expressions which describe their condition." The question had indeed "been most vehemently disputed and discussed, yet the Church was wisely silent, and allowed various mutually irreconcilable opinions to be held by her sons without rebuke. Neither at Nicea (A.D. 325), nor at Constantinople (A.D. 381), nor at Ephesus (A.D. 431), nor at Chalcedon (A.D. 451), was any special doctrine laid down respecting the future rewards and punishments, nor were the opinions of Origen and his followers on that subject condemned, or even alluded to."[1]

For many subsequent centuries "the dark shadow of Augustine" was thrown so powerfully over the current theology that there was little question about the endlessness of torment. They had however the developed doctrine of Purgatory, which alone helped the human conscience to dispense with Origen's theory of Restitution. The metaphysical grounds indeed on which the doctrine of endless torment was based were utterly inadequate and even absurd, as, for instance, that "offence against an Infinite Being must require an infinite penalty, and since a finite creature is not capable of punishment infinite in degree, *requiritur ut sit saltem duratione infinita."* This argument would require endless torment for any sin, even the most venial, and it tells quite as

---

[1] Rev. H. B. Wilson, *Speech*, p. 99.

strongly against any possibility of forgiveness on
this side of the grave. It is therefore *nihil ad rem;*
and the agonizing incidence of such a view was
lightened by the belief that all earthly sins could
be removed even *in articulo mortis* by priestly
absolution. They held, too, the doctrine of mitigation. "The punishment," says St. Thomas
Aquinas, "will not be absolutely removed, but
while it lasts pity will work by diminishing it." Still
it is to the Middle Ages and to scholastic theology
that we mainly owe the rigidity of the common
dogmas as to (1) the endlessness of doom, and
(2) its irreversibility after death. The extreme
confidence of the schoolmen, and their imaginary
knowledge of all the secrets of the other world,
might have taken warning from the passages in
which St. Gregory the Great (*De Vitâ aeternâ
Animarum,* iv. 40), after telling us a great deal
about purgatory, asks, " How so much was then
known about souls, when nothing had been been
known in earlier days?" and can furnish no

other answer than that the *futurum saeculum* becomes better known as the *praesens saeculum* draws to its conclusion.

From Gregory the Great till Anselm "the theology of Western Christendom slept her winter sleep." The sleep was "disturbed rather than broken by the strange apparition in the ninth century of Johannes Scotus Erigena, one of the most original thinkers of his own or any age, as of one born out of due time." [1] This brilliant and subtle metaphysician made future punishment consist only in the absence of divine bliss. " In igne aeterno nihil aliud esse poenam quam beatae felicitatis absentiam" (*De Praedest.* c. 16). Evil, being a mere negative conception, so also is punishment, and neither can be eternal. That which Christ has redeemed cannot be punished. The contradiction of this teaching to Scripture is, he says, merely apparent, and due to the finite character of human language. Bliss and pain

[1] H. N. Oxenham, *Catholic Doctrine of Atonement*, p. 63.

will be in the conscience only; fire, brimstone, &c.,
are but symbols meant to teach the dull imagination of the carnal. All things shall ultimately return to God. The distinction of sex
shall be abolished (Gal. iii. 28), heaven and earth
shall be all Paradise, and the creature shall be one
with the Creator. God shall be all in all (Scotus
Erig. *De Divis. Nat.* ii. 6; v. 8). "*Erit enim
Deus omnia in omnibus quando nihil erit nisi solus
Deus;*" and there shall be a *mirabilis atque ineffa-
bilis reversio* of human nature into God (pp.
232—234). He contrived to reconcile this with a
nominal acceptance of everlasting punishment by
saying that though all *malitia* will be abolished
its *phantasiae* in the conscience will remain; but in
v. 27, p. 260, he speaks with unmistakable clearness of the complete and final ἀποκατάστασις.

The Reformers mostly held to the old Augustinian conceptions, except in so far as they rejected
Purgatory. In the Augsburg Confession, art. 17,
we find "Damnant Anabaptistas, qui sentiunt

hominibus damnatis et diabolis finem poenarum futurum esse" (Cf. *Conf. Helvetic.* xi.). In fact (with the one exception already noted) they made but little change in the mediæval eschatology, which lay indeed beyond the range of the subjects with which they dealt. And if they intended to condemn the views of Origen, neither they nor the 42nd Article stated those views with any approach to accuracy. Abandoning the doctrine of the infallibility of the Church, they took refuge in the infallibility of Scripture, and, as is so often the case, this was extended into the infallibility of "the letter that killeth ;" and this, again, involved the infallibility of an exegesis which was yet in its merest infancy ; and worse still, the infallibility of all sorts of "private interpretations," such as no Scripture tolerates,[1] and respecting which no two sects or churches are thoroughly agreed. And yet the voice of reason and conscience, rising in revolt against a doctrine

---

[1] πᾶσα προϕητεία γραϕῆς ἰδίας ἐπιλύσεως οὐ γίνεται, 2 Pet. i. 20.

which they found irreconcilable with the love of God, still made itself occasionally heard, as in the writings of Eberhard, Basedow, Steinbart, and in Soner's *Demonstratio Theologica et Philosophica quod aeterna Impiorem Supplicia non arguant Dei Justitiam sed Injustitiam* (Altdorf), published posthumously in 1654.

In the course of years this revolt of the conscience against the tyrannous enforcement of a mere opinion has made itself so distinctly heard that Karl Hase (in his *Handbuch der Protest. Polemik*), pointing out that the Reformers did not follow up their negation by an affirmative doctrine, adds that the more scientific spirit of modern Protestantism has long ago observed this, and attached itself to the doctrine of the Alexandrians, and has acknowledged, in the other world also, the gracious government of God, and the "capability of development in the human spirit." Nothing will more imperil in devout and tender souls the entire system of Reformed theology

than this omission to state in its fullness the
Gospel of Hope; nothing will be a more potent
incentive to those who find the popular view
utterly intolerable, to find some alleviation from
its horror in the milder eschatology of the Church
of Rome for those within her pale.

It is needless to pursue this sketch any further.
The facts which I have adduced may be verified
by reference to the volumes of Baur, Hagenbach,
Haag, Gieseler, Neander, &c. Among those who
in recent days have inclined to some form of the
hope for which in these sermons I have been led
to plead are many illustrious names, of which none
is more illustrious than that of the great and saintly
Bengel. Others who may be mentioned are
Richard Clarke, Bishop Edmund Law, Bishop
Rust, William Law, Dr. Henry More, Dr. Thomas
Burnett, Chaplain to William III. (*De Statu
Mortuorum*, 1723), Henry Dodwell (*Epistolary
Discourses*, 1706), Bishop Newton, Dr. Chauncey
(1784), Rothe the eminent Lutheran divine (in his

Theologische Ethik), Neander, Oberlin, Tholuck, and Bishop Martensen of Seeland, the author of *Christliche Dogmatik*. There is in fact a distinct feeling among some of the ablest Protestant divines of Germany and of England that the bare negation of Purgatory by the Reformers left a void in doctrine which is perilous to all faith. Among recent defenders of this view we may mention Prof. Maurice, Dean Milman, Sir James Stephen, Lord Lyttleton, Canon Kingsley,[1] Thomas Erskine of Linlathen (in the second volume of whose letters may be found many noble and beautiful utterances on this subject), and Dr. Ewing, Bishop of Argyll and the Isles. Among illustrious prelates of our own Church, Archbishop Tillotson saw reason to believe that God might restore the lost by the superabundance of His mercy, though he considered that

---

[1] Canon Kingsley's opinions may be found in *The Water of Life*, p. 76, &c., and are repeatedly referred to in his Biography. It has been asserted that he abandoned these opinions. So far is this from being the case, that, had he lived, he intended to preach them with greater distinctness.

the letter of Scripture pointed the other way.
Archbishop Whately, like the learned Edmund
Law, Bishop of Carlisle, favoured the view of
Conditional Immortality.	This opinion, which
was also held by Dr. Watts and the late Isaac
Taylor, has been earnestly, but I cannot think
satisfactorily, maintained by many good men and
earnest Christians of our own day.	Bishop Thirl-
wall accepted with entire and warm approval that
hope of an amelioration, after death, of the state of
"spirits in prison" which is expressly involved in
our creed, and was treated with great force and
beauty in a sermon in St. Paul's Cathedral by my
friend Prof. Plumptre.	To Prof. Maurice, whom
all good and wise men honour, even when they
cannot agree with him—"quem nemo non parum
amat etiam qui plus amare non potest"—is due
the merit of restoring this precious hope.	The
present Archbishop of Canterbury, in his book
on the *Word of God and the Ground of Faith*,
speaks, if without sanction, yet without reproof,

of "a hope that, after the Day of Judgment, God's mercy may, in the lapse of infinite ages, find some mode of restoring the lost, consistently with the maintenance of His purity and justice."[1] The Archbishop of York, when he affirms (*Bampton Lectures*, p. 56) that "Life to the godless must be the beginning of destruction, since nothing but God and that which pleases Him can permanently exist," seems, intentionally or unintentionally, to favour the opinion of the ultimate annihilation of the wicked. Dr. Church, Dean of St. Paul's, in a sermon at Oxford, expresses views which obviously point in the same direction. "I should be disloyal," he says, "to Him whom I believe in and worship as the Lord of truth if I doubted that honest seeking would at last find Him. Even if it do not find Him here, man's destiny stops not at the grave, and many, we may be sure, will know Him there who did not know Him here." The Dean of Westminster, in his *Essays on Church and*

---

[1] Part ii. p. vi. Preface.

State and other writings, has given still firmer expression to the same hope. It was spoken of not
only with respect, but even with a sort of yearning
approval, as a view at least permissible, by Canon
Cook of Exeter—the editor of the *Speaker's Commentary*—in a sermon at Lincoln's Inn. Opinions
which, though they differ in detail, agree in the
utter repudiation of the popular theology, have
been openly maintained by the Rev. Prof. Birks
—a name so justly honoured among the English
Evangelicals; by the Rev. Professor Stokes—
whose scientific authority stands so high; by
the Rev. J. Ll. Davies; by the Revs. T. J.
Rowsell, Prof. Mayor, Canon Duckworth, and a
multitude of clergymen whose names are very
widely and honourably known. Were I at liberty
to mention the names of those high dignitaries
and eminent theologians whose view of the
subject is identical with my own, the position
which I have defended would be indefinitely
strengthened,—but this I will not do. Among

N

Nonconformists the same hopes have found eloquent and able supporters in the Rev. S. Cox,
author of *The Expositor's Notebook* and other
valuable works ; the Rev. J. Baldwin Brown,
President of the Independent Conference ; the
Rev. R. Dale ; the Rev. Dr. Parker ; the learned
and thoughtful Rev. Andrew Jukes (author of
The Restitution of all Things) ; and many others.
The opinion known as " conditional immortality "
has been earnestly and reverently supported by
the Rev. S. Minton (author of *The Glory of
Christ*); the Rev. J. B. Heard (author of *The
Tripartite Nature of Man*) ; the Rev. E. White
(author of *Life in Christ; or, Immortality peculiar to the Regenerate*) ; and an increasing number
of followers. I cannot, as I have said, accept this
view, but it seems to me far more in accordance
with the letter of Scripture, and far less shocking
to the moral sense than the crude dogmatism
which we hear so frequently about the endlessness
of material torments for the majority of mankind.

In the Roman Church an opinion akin to that of Origen is steadily gaining ground ; and it is stated by Dr. Cazenove in a letter to the *Guardian* (December, 1877) that Père Ravignan, the most eloquent French preacher of recent days, averred that it is the general doctrine among the Jesuits. This is at any rate a decisive proof that such a view is regarded as tenable in the Roman Church ;—which is equivalent to saying that the Catholic Church has never authoritatively decided the question. Even those Roman Catholics who accept the Augustinian view of endless torment (a view first *distinctly* formulated in the forged and malicious Clementines) yet frankly admit that doctrine of *refrigeria* and *mitigatio* even for the damned, which is as common in the Fathers as it was universal among the Rabbis, and which no œcumenical council has condemned.[1] Nor must it be forgotten that no member of

---

[1] See Petavius, *De Angelis*, quoted by Dr. Newman, *Grammar of Assent*, p. 317.

the Greek or Roman Church has to face in all their horrors the two doctrines which I impugn —of an irreversible doom passed at death, and of torment necessarily endless for every soul that has died in sin. The doctrine of an Intermediate State robs those popular conceptions of nine-tenths of their ghastliness, because it enables Christians to contemplate without agony the condition of all who are nearest and dearest to them, and practically of all who die with the last rites of their Church. It is quite true that of the doctrine of Purgatory, in the precise and dogmatic form of it, there is no adequate proof; but the expression of our Article, "a fond thing vainly invented," applies, I imagine, far less to the mere doctrine than to the mass of flagrant abuses with which it had become inevitably identified.[1] "That dragon's tail, the mass," said Luther, "begot multiplied abominations. First Purgatory," which

[1] "The primitive doctrine is not condemned in the Article (22nd), unless indeed the doctrine be Romish, *which must not be supposed.*" —Dr. Newman, Tract., p. 23.

with all pertaining to it, he proceeds to call a mere devil's mask (*mera diaboli larva est*), *Art. Smalcald*, p. 307. But in point of fact the taunt of the Romish controversialist, Möhler, that 'Protestanism must either admit many into heaven stained with sin, or imagine that a magical change is wrought merely by death,' is unanswerable, unless we reply with Karl Hase that both views are untenable, since most men at death are indeed not wicked enough to deserve an endless hell, yet not holy enough to be admitted into heaven. And Hase proceeds to argue with justice that our Protestantism is perfectly reconcilable (not indeed with a dogmatic and definite) but with "a subdued and enlightened view of purgatory," *i.e.* of progressive amelioration, of a purifying process, after death.

Lastly, as in no one of the Catholic Creeds of Christendom is endless damnation, with its accessories, made an article of faith,—though every creed expresses that unlimited faith in "the forgiveness of sins" which is the chief hope of life, and the richest blessing of immortality,—so by no single formulary of the Church of England is such a dogma required. In the case of Fendall *v.* Wilson, 1863-4, the Judicial Committee of the Privy Council, with the concurrence of, and without protest from, the late Archbishop of Canterbury and the present Archbishops of Canterbury and York, decided[1] that "we do not find in the formularies[2] to which this Article" [a charge that Mr. Wilson had denied the endlessness of future punishment] "refers, any such distinct declaration of our Church upon the subject as to require us to condemn as penal the expression of hope by a clergyman that even the ultimate pardon of the wicked, who are condemned in the day of judgment, may be consistent with the will of God." For ten years indeed (1552—1561) a Forty-second Article condemned Universalism ; but

---

[1] Brooke's *Privy Council Judgments*, p. 102.

[2] Among which were the damnatory clauses of the Athanasian Creed.

for Universalism I have not pleaded, and, moreover, even that Article was struck out with the
consent of the Bishops and Clergy of both Houses
and both provinces. To say that it was struck
out because the Anabaptists were no longer prominent is simply an unsupported conjecture. The
conjecture may be true, but even if so I look
on the elimination of the Article as distinctly
overruled by a watchful Providence ; since it
is the province of the Church to decide only in
matters of *faith*, and no Church has a right to
legislate in these matters of *opinion* on which
wise and holy men have, in all ages, been content
to differ, seeing that we have no indisputable voice
of Revelation to guide our conclusions respecting
them.

EXCURSUS I., p. xlv.

THE TEACHING OF BISHOP BUTLER ON THE FUTURE LIFE.

I AM permitted to print the following valuable and important letter, which reached me after I had written the remarks in the text. It will be observed that the passage which I have quoted is one more to be added to those so strikingly combined by Professor Plumptre ; and I hope that the great name of Bishop Butler will no longer be abused in support of views which he has nowhere maintained, which he evidently regarded as very dubious, and which—had he lived in these days—he would almost certainly have repudiated with still greater distinctness. With every word that Bishop Butler has written on the subject I heartily agree :—

BICKLEY VICARAGE,
Christmas, December, 1877.

MY DEAR FARRAR,

The passage in Butler's *Analogy* to which I referred as bearing on the great question with which you have been led to deal is in Part i. c. 3.

" Virtue, to borrow the Christian allusion, is militant here, and various untoward accidents contribute to its being often overborne : but it may *combat* with greater advantage hereafter, and prevail completely, and enjoy its consequent rewards in some future states. Neglected as it is, perhaps unknown, perhaps despised and oppressed here, there may be scenes in eternity lasting enough, and in

every way adapted to afford it a sufficient sphere of action ; and a
sufficient sphere for the natural consequences of it to follow in fact.
. . . . And, one might add, that suppose all this advantageous tendency of virtue to become effect amongst one or more orders of
vicious creatures in any distant scene or period throughout the universal
kingdom of God ; *this happy effect of virtue would have a tendency
by way of example, and possibly in other ways, to amend those of
them who are capable of amendment* and being recovered to a just
sense of virtue.   If our notions of the plan of Providence were enlarged in any sense proportionable to what late discoveries have
enlarged our views with respect to the material world, representations of this kind would not appear absurd or extravagant."

It seems to me that these remarkable words throw light on the
teaching of the previous chapter, in which Butler dwells very solemnly
on the warning thought, suggested by the natural course of things,
that the punishment of evil-doers may, if the evil has reached a
certain measure, be final and irreversible.   He holds very strongly
the truth that this life is a state of probation, and that after it each
man will receive according to his deeds, and "in *exact proportion* to
the good or evil which he has done."   He does not deal directly with
the problems presented by cases in which, as with infants, idiots,
and, we must add, the vast multitudes who have lived and died in
the times of ignorance, there has been no real probation.   He enters
his protest against those who "forget or explain away, after ac-
knowledging it in words," the truth that "every one shall be
equitably dealt with."   He maintains that "all shadow of injustice,
and indeed all harsh appearances, in this various economy of Providence would be lost if we would keep in mind that every merciful
allowance shall be made, and no more be required of any one than
what might have been equitably expected of him, from the circumstances in which he was placed." (Part. ii. c. 6.) He expressly protests

(Part. ii. chap. v., note F) against the dogma that "none can have the benefit of the general redemption, but such as have the advantage of being made acquainted with it in the present life." He describes that redemption as "an interposition to prevent the destruction of human kind, *whatever that destruction unprevented would have been.*"

It is clear, I think, from these passages (1) That Butler rejected the mediæval dogmatism, which, following Augustine, limited salvation to the baptised, and (2) the more or less prevalent Protestant dogmatism which limits it to those who know and believe in Christ. (3) That he carefully avoids pronouncing on the nature of the future punishments of evil, and never from first to last dwells on the pictures of material horrors in which so many have delighted. (4) That looking to the whole drift of his argument that future rewards and punishments come by general laws, and as the natural consequences of the good or bad deeds to which they are attached (Part i. chap. 3; Part ii. chap. 1), it is probable, from the *Analogy*, that he thought of the latter as consisting mainly in the "uneasiness, disturbance, apprehension, shame," which follow on evil now, and will hereafter be felt with a new and terrible intensity: just as in Sermon xiv. he dwells with what is, for him, a marvellous eloquence on the blessedness of the saints as consisting in "the perception of God's presence with us in a nearer and stricter way" than is now possible. But the passage with which I began this letter opens, I think, a wider view. There is, from Butler's point of view, a field for "*combat*" after death as well as now. There are, or may be, "*orders of vicious creatures*" in God's kingdom who may yet be "*capable of amendment, and of being recovered to a just sense of virtue.*" And in yet another passage (Part i. chap. 5) we have the same thought developed. "Nothing which we at present see

would lead us to the thought of a solitary unactive life hereafter."
Analogy and Scripture alike teach us that "it will be a community."
For aught we know, the life of that community may "give scope
for the exercise of *veracity, justice,* and *charity.*"

Combine this passage with the other, and is not the inference
almost irresistible that Butler was tentatively feeling after, and all
but absolutely grasping, the truth that the energies of the saints made
perfect will be, as analogy suggests, exerted in the same direction
and for the same ends as they are now on earth?   And if the highest
object of such energies now be to rescue those who are perishing
from lack of knowledge, and who yet are capable of recovery, then
the whole drift of the argument of the *Analogy* suggests the continuance of that highest energy in the unknown spheres of action after
death.   I have ventured to express that thought in some lines in
memory of one who occupied a high place in the lot of the saintly
sufferers of whom the world knows little, and they are, I think, in
harmony with Butler's teaching.

He, too, is there ; and can we dream
    Their joy is other now than when
    They dwelt among the sons of men,
As walking in the Eternal gleam?

Are there no souls behind the veil
    That need the help of guiding hand ;
    Weak hearts that cannot understand
Why earth's poor dreams of Heaven must fail?

Are there no prison-doors to ope,
    No lambs to gather in the fold,
.   No treasure-house of new and old,
To meet each wish and crown each hope?

We know not : but if life be there
The outcome and the crown of this,
What else can make their perfect bliss
Than in the Master's work to share ?

Resting, but not in slumbrous ease,
Working, but not in wild unrest,
Still ever blessing, ever blest,
They see us, as the Father sees.

The view thus suggested by the *Analogy* is, as might be expected, wiser and deeper than Paley's rough and ready way of
dealing with this great question ; but his words too are worth
quoting as showing how his robust practical sense of justice shrank
from the common forms either of mediæval or Protestant dogmatism on this matter. "It has been said, that it can never be
a just economy of Providence to admit one part of mankind into
heaven and condemn the other to hell, since there must be very
little to choose between the worst man who is received into heaven
and the best who is excluded. And how know we, it might be
answered, but that there may be as little to choose in their conditions? "—*Moral Philosophy*, Book i. Ch. 7.

You will see that I have confined myself to the task which I had
undertaken of clearing the teaching of Butler from prevalent mis-
conceptions. I will not enter into any full discussion of the whole
question. I have not shrunk from placing before those who care to
know, what I hold and teach as to its momentous issues. Now in
one form, now in another, I have endeavoured to show that a wider
hope than that of mediæval Catholicism or popular Protstantism is
in harmony with the analogy of Nature, with the teaching of Scripture, with the thoughts of the " masters of those who know " in the

Christian Church.   I have not read your sermons, and do not know
how far I should accept your conclusions, or how far you adopt mine.
But as this letter is to be printed with them, and as you tell me that
you wish to connect my name with the volume—an honour which,
on personal grounds, as having been once the master of a scholar
from whom I have since been glad to learn, I have thankfully
accepted—I think it may be well to make my own position
clear by stating, without discussing, the conclusions to which I have
been led.

On the one hand, I have never been able, in spite of the apparent sanction given to it by such passages as Rom. xi. 32, v. 19, 20,
Isaiah liii. 11, to accept the theory of Universalism ; (2) I have as
little been able to accept the theory of Annihilation as the ultimate
portion of all but the elect in Christ.   It seems to me to have no
grounds in Scripture, or reason, or the analogy of Nature, and to be
at variance with our fundamental conceptions, as shown in the
consensus of mankind, as to the soul's immortality ; (3) I have never
been able to attach any great importance to the discussions that have
turned upon the meaning of the word αἰώνιος.   I cannot, on philological grounds, agree with Mr. Maurice in thinking that our Lord's
teaching in John xvii. 3, excludes from it the idea of duration,
and the whole history of the word shows that it cannot, as a
word, denote endlessness.   (4) I do not hesitate, however, to accept
the thought of the punishment of evil as being endless.   If that
punishment comes, as Butler teaches us, as the "natural consequence"
of sin, if the enduring pain be

> "Memory of evil seen at last
> As evil, hateful, loathsome,"

then I cannot see how it can be otherwise than everlasting.   Christian theology knows no water of Lethe to steep the soul in forget-
fulness of its own past ; and if the sin is not forgotten, then the

remembrance of it must throughout the ages be an element of; pain and sorrow. Experience, indeed, teaches that the penitent, in whom that sorrow is keenest, finds it not incompatible with peace and joy even now, and the extension of that experience beyond the veil suggests the thought that there may be a retributive element mingling with the blessedness of the highest saints; and, by parity of reason, as in the view maintained by Mr. Birks, Mr. E. H. Bickersteth, and substantially by Mr. Erskine of Linlathen, that the acceptance of the punishment, the admission that it is inseparable from the righteousness of God, may bring hereafter, as it brings with it now, a mitigation of the anguish. (5) While I reject the Romish, and even the Augustinian view of Purgatory, as not only without any certain warranty of Scripture, but as a "fond thing vainly invented," resting on the radically false conception that a quantitative amount of physical pain has in itself any power to purify the soul from a proportionate quantity of evil deeds or their results, I hold that it is at variance with our belief in the eternal love and righteousness of God to assume that any created will can be fixed in evil by a divine decree, coming at the close of a few months or years of an imperfect probation, and therefore that Scripture, and reason, and analogy alike lead to the belief that we must supplement the idea of probation by that of a discipline and education which is begun in this life, often with results that seem to us as failure and a hopeless waste, but to which, when we look before and after, we can assign no time-limits. The will, in the exercise of its imperishable gift of freedom, may frustrate that education hereafter, as it frustrates it here; but if it does so, it is because it "kicks against the pricks" of the long-suffering that is leading it to repentance; and there, as here, it may accept even an endless punishment, and find peace in the acceptance. Lastly, I will quote words which seem to me to go almost to the root of the whole matter, and which need only to be extended beyond the limits that the narrowing system to which the writer has bound himself attaches to them, to be the last words that I need now write on this great question.

> " And these two pains so counter and so keen,
>   The longing for Him when thou seest Him not,
>   The shame of self at thought of seeing Him,
>   Shall be thy keenest, sharpest Purgatory."
>   J. H. Newman, *Dream of Gerontius.*

I am,

Ever yours affectionately,

E. H. PLUMPTRE.

ON THE TRANSLATIONS OF κρίνειν AND ῞Αιδης, &c.

Nothing that I have said seems to have excited stranger misapprehension and anger than the statement of this plain, indisputable fact, which no scholar in England will dream of denying, and to which one of our most learned prelates has referred in his last charge. "Such instances as the following," says Dr. Jacobson, Bishop of Chester,—in a charge delivered only last month, and which came into my hands after my sermon had been preached, —"*must* be allowed to go some way towards justifying a desire for further revision.

" The confusion of *Hades* with *Gehenna*.

" The modification which some words undergo by lapse of time, *e.g. damnation.*" P. 30.

A reviser may indeed choose to consider that κρίνειν and κατακρίνειν mean the same as "damn," though then, as Mr. Ruskin has pointed out, he should render it by this word throughout, and we should have such verses as " Woman, where are those thine accusers? hath no man damned thee?" &c., and he may consider that "Hell" connotes the same thing as γέεννα ; and that αἰώνιος is identical sometimes with never-ending ; and, therefore, that these notions may be introduced in a few texts, though it is impossible to introduce them into all or most. But, even if he holds such entirely untenable views—and it is quite certain that the majority, at any rate, of our own Revisers are far too wise and too learned to do so— he would still have no right to obtrude his private opinion when by a confessedly *faithful* translation, which prejudges no controversy, he can render the Greek words by "*judgment* " and " *condemnation ;*" by " *Hades,*" " *Gehenna,*" and, in one place, " *Tartarus ;* " and by " *eternal.*" And this, if I mistake not, is what will actually be done.

O

I. The facts are these. In the New Testament the words κρίνω, κρίσις, and κρίμα occur some 190 times ; the words κατακρίνω, κατάκρισις, κατάκριμα occur twenty-four times, and yet there are *only fifteen places* out of more than 200 in which our translation has *deviated from the proper renderings of "judge" and "condemn," into "damn" and its cognates.* It is singular that they should have used " damnation " only for the milder words κρίσις and κρίμα.

This single fact ought to be decisive to every candid mind ; but it is worth while to point out how disastrous—how more than disastrous, how *fatal*—in some passages that divergence has been.

a. 2. Pet. ii. 1. " Damnable heresies " should be " heresies of destruction " (ἀπωλείας), *i.e.* destructive heresies. The inaccurate rendering has done much to add fuel to the already too fierce fires of intolerance. The same remark applies to 2 Thess. ii. 12, where "all might be damned" is " may be judged " (κριθῶσι).

β. Matt. xxiii. 13, Mark xii. 40, Luke xx. 47. " Ye (they) shall receive *the greater damnation.*" Our Lord used no such words. He said περισσότερον κρίμα, "a severer judgment."

γ. Matt. xxiii. 33. " How shall ye escape *the damnation of hell ?*" What Christ said was something utterly different,—"the judgment of Gehenna."

δ. Mark iii. 29. " Is in danger of eternal damnation." What Christ said was " shall be liable to, shall incur the risk of—æonian sin " (*leg.* ἁμαρτήματος).

ε. Mark xvi. 16. " But he that believeth not shall be damned." What Christ said was " but, disbelieving, he shall be condemned." (Further, the passage is of dubious authenticity.)

ζ. John v. 29. " They that have done evil to the resurrection of *judgment*" (κρίσεως, not even κατακρίματος). The English version is here just as little justifiable as if in Matt. x. 15, &c., it had spoken of "the day of damnation."

η. No less disastrous in their consequences are some of these renderings in St. Paul's Epistles. In Rom. iii. 8 render "whose judgment (κρίσις) is just" In Rom. xiii. 2 render "they shall receive to themselves judgment" (κρίσιν).

θ. In 1 Cor. xi. 29 who would imagine that St. Paul meant that every unworthy communicant eats and drinks "*damnation*" to himself? How many have been utterly terrified from the blessings of the Holy Communion, and have therefore been robbed of the highest means of spiritual grace by the deplorable reproduction of this mistranslation in our Communion Service? All that St. Paul said was that a man who eats and drinks unworthily, by not discriminating the Lord's body, eats and drinks *judgment* to himself (κρίμα). On the shipwreck of sense caused by obliterating the distinctions of κρίνω, διακρίνω, κατακρίνω in this passage, see Lightfoot *On Revision*, p. 85.

ι. 1. Tim. v. 12. Why are English readers left unprotected to the dreadful perversion involved in saying that young widows who marry again "have *damnation*," whereas in vs. 14 he *recommends* them to do so? St. Paul merely says "incurring judgment," which is perhaps explicable by 1 Cor. vii. 28, 40.

κ. Rom. xiv. 23. "He that doubteth *is damned* if he eat"—*i.e.* damned for neglecting the mere scruple of a weak conscience! St. Paul says that if a man does not judge himself (ὁ μὴ κρίνων ἑαυτόν) in that which he alloweth he is happy; but if he eats *in spite of* a distinct scruple, he has been condemned (κατακέκριται),—obviously by his own conscience.

II. Of the renderings of Hades, Tartarus, and Gehenna, I have already spoken in the preface,[1] and will here only repeat that "hell" has entirely changed its old harmless sense of "the dim underworld,'[2] and that meaning as it now does to myriads of readers, "a

---

[1] See too Lightfoot *On Revision*, p. 79.

[2] "*Helan*" is "to cover." Archbishop Usher says that in Ireland "to *hell* the head" s to cover the head, and a *hellier* is a slater. In Hudibras the word is used for the place where the tailor throws his shreds. The word must have

place of endless torment by material fire into which all impenitent souls pass for ever after death,"—it conveys meanings which are not to be found in any word of the Old or New Testament for which it is presented as an equivalent. In our Lord's language Capernaum was to be thrust down not "to hell," but to the silence and desolation of the grave (Hades); the promise that "the gates of Hades" should not prevail against the Church is perhaps a distinct implication of her triumph even beyond death in the souls of men for whom He died; Dives uplifts his eyes, not "in hell," but in the intermediate Hades, where he rests till the resurrection to a judgment, in which signs are not wanting that his soul may meanwhile have been ennobled and purified. The "damnation of hell" is the very different "judgment of Gehenna;" and hell-fire is the "Gehenna of fire," an expression which on Jewish lips was *never* applied in our Lord's days to endless torment. Our translators are not, of course, responsible for the inferences drawn from words which have, since their day, changed their meaning; but our Revisers will be certain to bear in mind that "a good translator scrupulously abstains from introducing ideas of which the original contains no trace."[1]

Of "everlasting" I have spoken in the next Excursus.

begun to assume its darkest sense in 1611, or the translators would not have altered "O Hell, where is thy victory?" 1 Cor. xv. 55.

[1] Origen tells us (*c. Cels*. vi. 25) that finding the word "Gehenna" in the Gospels for the place of punishment, he made a special search into its meaning and history; and after mentioning (1) the valley of Hinnom, and (2) a *purificatory* fire (εἰς τὴν μετὰ βασάνων κάθαρσιν), he mysteriously adds that he thinks it unwise to speak without reserve about his discoveries. No one reading the passage can doubt that he means to imply the use of the word "Gehenna" among the Jews to indicate a *terminable*, and not an endless punishment. And he says in round terms that Celsus and others talked of "Gehenna" in total ignorance of its real meaning; in which they have had many followers.

EXCURSUS III. (p. 79).

The word "æonian," though sanctioned by Mr. Tennyson in the lines—

> " Draw down æonian hills, and sow
> The dust of continents to be,"

and though rendered very desirable by the sad confusion of eternity with the mere negative conception of endlessness, can perhaps hardly be naturalised. It is not worth while once more to discuss its meaning when it has been so ably proved by so many writers that there is *no authority whatever for rendering it "everlasting,"* and when even those who, like Dr. Pusey, are such earnest defenders of the doctrine of an endless hell, yet admit that the word only means "endless within the sphere of its own existence," so that on their own showing the word does not prove their point, and is, for instance, powerless against those who hold the doctrine of Conditional Immortality.

It may be worth while, however, to point out once more to less educated readers that αἰών, αἰώνιος, and their Hebrew equivalents in all combinations are *repeatedly* used of things which *have come and shall come to an end.* Even Augustine admits (what, indeed, no one can deny) that in Scripture αἰών, αἰώνιος must in many instances mean "having an end ;" and St. Gregory of Nyssa, who at least knew Greek, uses αἰώνιος as the epithet of "an interval."

Thus in the Old Testament αἰών, αἰώνιος, and many such varieties of expression as εἰς αἰῶνα αἰῶνος, &c., which with the Hebrew expressions like לְעוֹלָם or לְעוֹלָם וָעֶד (ἐπ' αἰῶνα καὶ ἔτι, in sæculum et ultra, "for ever and beyond!") are in our version rendered "for ever," or "for ever and ever"; but so far from necessarily implying *endlessness*, they are used of many Jewish ordinances which ceased centuries ago, such as the sprinkling of the lintel at the Passover (Ex. xii. 24), the Aaronic priesthood and its institutions (xxix. 9 ; xl. 15 ; Lev. iii. 17 ; Numb. xviii. 19) ; the inheritance given to Caleb (Josh. xiv. 9) ; Solomon's temple (1. Kings viii. 12, 13) ; the period of a slave's life (Deut. xv. 17, Job xli. 4) ; the burning of the fire upon the altar ("The fire shall ever be burning upon the altar; it shall never go out," Lev. vi. 13, &c.) ; and the leprosy of Gehazi (2 Kings v. 27). How purely figurative these phrases are may be seen by such passages as the following :—"The land thereof shall become burning pitch. It shall not be quenched night or day ; the smoke thereof shall go up *for ever*" (Is. xxxiv. 9, 10). And so fully is this a recognised idiom that in Deut. xxiii. 3, 6, we find "*for ever*" put side by side with "till the tenth generation ;" and though it is added "thou shalt not seek their peace and prosperity *for ever*," yet of the very Moabites and Ammonites of whom this is spoken we find a prophesy of peace and comfort in Jer. xlviii. 47 ; xlix. 6.

That the adjective αἰώνιος is applied to some things which are "endless" does not of course for one moment prove that the word itself meant "endless ;" and to introduce this rendering into many passages would be utterly impossible and absurd. To translate it in a few passages by "everlasting," when in the large majority of passages it is rendered "eternal," is a purely wanton and arbitrary variation, which unhappily occurs in one and the same verse (Matt. xxv. 46).

Our translators have naturally shrunk from such a phrase as "the endless God." The utter dearth of metaphysical knowledge renders most people incapable of realising a condition which is independent of time—a condition which crushes eternity into an hour, and extends an hour into eternity. But the philosophic Jews and the greatest Christian Fathers were quite familiar with it. "Æon," says Philo, "is the life of God, and is not time, but the archetype of time, and in it there is neither past, nor present, nor future."[1]

In answer to the old argument invented by St. Augustine,— ("Dicere autem in hoc uno eodemque sensu, vita aeterna sine fine erit, supplicium aeternum finem habebit, multum absurdum est," *De Civ. Dei* xxi. 23),—and since his day so incessantly repeated,— the argument, namely, that if we do not make αἰώνιος κόλασις mean endless punishment, we have no security that αἰώνιος ζωή means endless life, and that we thus lose our promise of everlasting happiness, I reply—

1. That this is absolutely no argument whatever, and ought never to be heard again, because the very men who most insist upon it contemptuously set it aside if we ask them to apply identically the same argument, analogously, to such texts as "As in Adam 'all' die, even so in Christ shall 'all' be made alive."

2. That our sure and certain hope of everlasting happiness rests on no such miserable foundation as the disputed meaning of a Greek adjective which is used over and over again of things transitory. If we need texts on which to rest it we may find plenty, such as Luke xx. 36, Hos. xiii. 14, Rev. xxi. 4, Is. xxv. 8, 1 Cor. xv. *passim*, &c.

3. That although we take the word αἰώνιος in both clauses to mean "eternal"—by which (in this connection) we mean *something*

[1] Philo. ὅτι ἀτρεπτὸν τὸ θεῖον, ed. Mangey. i. 277 ; *De Nom. Mutat. ad fin* (Mangey. i. 619) ; Greg. Naz. *Orat.* 38, "What to us is time, measured by the motion of the sun, is to the Immortals the Æon."—See Ecclus. xviii. 8—11.

above and beyond time, time being simply a mode of thought necessary only to our finite condition—(See John v. 39, xvii. 3)—yet it is
by no means necessarily the case that the word should have identically the same meaning in both clauses, since the meaning of
the same adjective might quite conceivably be modified, and even
altered, by that of the substantive to which it is attached. Nothing
could be more in accordance with the ordinary genius of human
speech than that the same adjective might have its fullest meaning in
one clause, in which that meaning is entirely consonant with reason
and conscience, yet not have it in the other, where it would
be shocking and terrible. What makes the argument as absolutely inexcusable on philological as it is on all other grounds, is that
in Rom. xvi. 25, 26, this very word occurs twice, and in one of the
two clauses *cannot* mean "everlasting," since it is speaking of time
which has come to an end ; and is yet translated "everlasting" by
our translators in the very next clause !—"According to the revelation of a mystery hidden in silence in the *eternal times*"
(E.V. "before the world began," where the reader will see that
"endless" would be a flagrant absurdity), "but now made manifest
according to the command of the Eternal God."

4. That in this instance the substantive κόλασις is a word which
in its *sole* proper meaning "has reference to the correction and
bettering of him that endures" (see *Philo. Leg. ad Cai.* 1). So
that Clement of Alexandria "defines κυλάσεις as μερικαὶ παιδεῖαι."
Archbishop Trench does indeed remark (*New Test. Synonyms,*
p. 30) that "It would be a very serious error to transfer this distinction (of κόλασις and τιμωρία) to the words as employed in the
New Testament." Why should it be a *serious error* to refrain from
reading into a word a sense which it does not possess? According
to Aristotle κόλασις is corrective, τιμωρία alone is vindictive ; κόλασις
has in view the improvement of the offender, τιμωρία the satisfaction

of the inflictor (ἡ μὲν κόλασις τοῦ πάσχοντος ἕνεκά ἐστιν· ἡ δε τιμωρία τοῦ ποιοῦντος ἵνα ἀποπληρωθῇ,—*Rhet.* i. 10, 17). It is Josephus, not our Lord and His Apostles, who use such phrases as ἀθάνατος τιμωρία and εἰργμός ἀΐδιος ; and though "everlasting death" occurs in our Liturgy, it nowhere occurs in Scripture, frequently as we read of æonian life.

5. But surely there are other grounds on which we ought to have heard the last of this dreary argument, to which it is hardly possible to listen without indignation. Good men, from St. Augustine to St. Thomas Aquinas (*Summ.* part iii., *Suppl. Quaest.* 99, iii.), and from St. Thomas to Dr. Pusey, have gone on repeating it *ad nauseam,* and even the gentle Keble wrote—

" And if the treasures of Thy wrath could waste,
Thy lovers must their promised heaven forego."

We hear the question asked triumphantly in sermons, "If the punishment of the wicked is not to last for ever, what guarantee have we that the felicity of the blessed will last for ever?" I reply, Is there not in the question—when not traditionally repeated, but plainly considered—an intense selfishness and a most ignoble thought of God?

Thank God, my own hopes of seeing God's face for ever hereafter do not rest on ten times refuted attempts to read false meanings into the Greek lexicon, in order to support a system far darker than St. Augustine's, from whose mistaken literalism it took its disastrous origin. But here I declare, and call God to witness, that if the popular doctrine of Hell were true I should be ready to resign all hope, not only of a *shortened* but of *any* immortality, if thereby I could save, not *millions,* but *one single human soul* from what fear, and superstition, and ignorance, and inveterate hate, and slavish letter-worship, have dreamed and taught of Hell. I call God to

witness that so far from regretting the possible loss of some billions
of æons of bliss by attaching to the word αἰώνιος a sense in which
scores of times it is undeniably found, I would here, and now, and
kneeling on my knees, ask Him that I might die as the beasts that
perish, and for ever cease to be, rather than that my worst enemy
should endure the hell described by Tertullian, or Minucius Felix, or
Jonathan Edwards, or Dr. Pusey, or Mr. Furniss, or Mr. Moody, or
Mr. Spurgeon, for one single year. Unless my whole nature were
utterly changed, I can imagine no immortality which would not be
abhorrent to me if it were accompanied with the knowledge that
millions and millions and millions of poor suffering wretches—some
of whom on earth I had known and loved—were writhing in an
agony without end or hope.[1]

[1] It may be worth while to add these further notes about αἰών. Heyschius
says it is sometimes used for " a long time ;" and Origen alludes to the same fact.
In Exod. Hom. vi. 13; περὶ ὁρχῶν, ii. 3, 5. Leontius Byzantinus, even in
arguing against Origenists, admits that both in profane and sacred literature
αἰών is used of a definite period (περὶ ἀρισμένου χρόνου λαμβίνεται).
Caesarius (*Dial.* 3) even observes that the Origenist argument on the terminability
of torment was derived from the use of this very word ! Huetius, *Origeniana*
(*Opp. ed.* Paris, iv. pp. 211, 233).

EXCURSUS IV. (p. 64).

"For my part I fancy I should not grieve if the whole race of mankind died in its fourth year. As far as we can see I do not know that it would be a thing much to be lamented."—Henry Rogers (Greyson's *Letters*, i. 34).

"In the distress and anguish of my own spirit I confess that I see no light whatever. I see not one ray to disclose to me the reason why sin came into the world, why the earth is strewed with the dying and the dead, and why man must suffer to all eternity."— Albert Barnes, *Practical Sermons*, p. 123.

"Were it possible for man's imagination to conceive the horrors of such a doom as this, all reasoning about it would be at an end, it would scorch and wither all the power of human thought."— Archer Butler's *Sermons* (second series), p. 383.

"The same gospel which penetrates our soul with warm emotions, dispersive of selfishness, brings in upon the heart a sympathy that tempts us often to wish that itself were not true, or that it had not taught us so to feel."—Isaac Taylor, *Restoration of Belief*, p. 367.

> "As being that had burned
> Half an eternity, and was to burn
> For evermore he looked. O sight to be
> Forgotten, though too terrible to think !"
>
> Pollok, *Course of Time.*

"Far be it from us to make light of the demerit of sin. . . . But still what is man?" (After dwelling on his corrupt nature, his weakness, his ignorance, the strength of his passions and appetites, and the short sinful course of his few fleeting years on earth, he adds—) "But endless punishment! Hopeless misery through a duration to which the terms above imagined will be absolutely nothing! I acknowledge my *inability* (I would say reverently) to admit this belief together with a belief in the divine goodness—the belief that 'God is love,' that 'His tender mercies are over all His works.'"—John Foster, *On Future Punishment.*

"O most tender heart of Jesus, why wilt Thou not end, when wilt Thou end, this ever-growing horror of sin and woe? When wilt Thou chase away the devil into his own hell, and close the pit's mouth, that Thy chosen may rejoice in Thee, quitting the thoughts of those who perish in their wilfulness?"—J. H. Newman, *Discourses.*

"Decretum *horribile* fateor."—Calvin, *Instt.*

I have said that the doctrine, as commonly taught, is a fruitful source of scepticism :—

"L'Eglise Romaine s'est porté le dernier coup : elle a consommé son suicide le jour ou elle a fait Dieu implacable et la damnation éternelle."—George Sand, *Spiridion*, p. 302.

"If this be the logical result of accepting theories, better believe in no God at all."—Leslie Stephen, *English Thought in Eighteenth Century.*

THE VOICE OF SCRIPTURE RESPECTING ETERNAL HOPE.

Before adducing the various passages of Scripture which are here referred to, I may make one or two observatio. s respecting them.

I. In proportion to the deep and unfeigned reverence which I have ever felt for Holy Scripture, is the sense of sorrow, and almost of indignation, with which I view its constant perversion by the attempt to build up infinite systems out of metaphorical ex-pressions and isolated texts. I have spoken of this terrible abuse in one of my sermons ; and I have said elsewhere that we must be guided, not by texts torn from their context, but by the whole scope and tenor of revelation. Texts have been perverted from the earliest times to the most unworthy purposes. They have—to the deadly injury of the divine authority of Scripture—been quoted for centuries in the cause of ignorance and sin. They have been abused, by the endless errors of private interpretation, to countenance every absurdity, and check every science, and denounce every moral reformation. They were quoted against Columbus, against Coper-nicus, against Galileo, against the geologists. They were quoted against St. Peter, against St. Paul, nay, even against Christ Him-self. They were quoted against Wycliffe, against Luther, against Wilberforce, against the cause of Education, against the cause of

Temperance. They have been quoted in defence of polygamy, in defence of oppression, in defence of persecution, in defence of intolerance, in defence of "the right divine of kings to govern wrong."
I care but little in any controversy for the stress laid on one or two
isolated and dubious texts out of the sacred literature of fifteen
hundred years. They may be torn from their context ; they may
be distorted ; they may be misinterpreted ; they may be irrelevant ;
they may be misunderstood ; they may—as the Prophets and the
Apostles and our Blessed Lord Himself distinctly intimated—
they may reflect the ignorance of a dark age or the fragment of
an imperfect revelation ; they may be a bare concession to imperfection, or a low steppingstone to progress. What the Bible
teaches as a whole—what the Bibles also teach as a whole—for
History, and Conscience, and Nature, and Experience—these too
are Sacred Books,—that, and that only, is the immutable law of
God.[1]

II. Now if the doctrine of endless torment, with all its Calvinis-
tic and popular accretions, be true, it is incredible that there should
be no trace of it in the entire Old Testament,[2] except by putting on

---

[1] Two writers, with neither of whom I agree, but who are distinguished by the
most devout reverence for the Word of God in Holy Scripture, have recently
expressed similar thoughts. "The Bible," says Mr. White, "has fallen much
into the hands of those who imagine that a few favourite 'texts' will suffice to
prove that Omniscience is on the side of even the most extravagant theologies.
The world has already suffered too much from *systems founded on* a handful of
wrested quotations, to allow of much reticence in repudiating those hermen-
eutical methods" (*Life in Christ*, p. 3,8). "The Gospel," says Mr. Minton,
"saves by the revelation which it makes of the heart and mind of God," and when
we are faced by such a doctrine as "endless torment," is it unnatural to "inquire
whether there may not be some mistake in the common interpretation of the four
or five passages which are thought to attribute such an intention to the Creator?"

[2] Dan. xii. 2—to say nothing of the fact that it only says "*many* of them
that sleep," and that the word rendered "everlasting" does not mean "everlast-

the Hebrew phrase "for ever" a sense which it cannot and does not bear. Those who insist on doing this put themselves at once out of court as incompetent and biassed critics. Nor can anything more forcibly illustrate what I have said on the reckless abuse of texts than the ignorant persistence with which such passages as Is. xxiii. 14, or Eccl. xi. 3, are urged in favour of endless torments, with which they have not the very remotest connection.

III. I have already stated that the Jews, studying the Old Testament without any polemical bias about this subject, and with every temptation to interpret every passage of it in the darkest sense which might gratify their passionate, and not unnatural, indignation against a world which has treated them with such unbounded cruelty and scorn, have yet never held or taught the doctrine of endless torment as any part of their religion. I have consulted Rabbi H. N. Adler on this subject, and in his very full and courteous reply he assures me that "the Jews do not possess any authorised dogmatic teaching on the subject of endless punishment; and that the views of each rabbi depended on his interpretation of the several Scripture texts bearing upon this point and upon the results of his own reflection and investigation." I have referred to the principal passages of the Talmud bearing upon the question. There are two *loci classici.*

Rosh Hashana, p. 17.—"But unbelievers, &c., go down into Gehenna and are adjudged therein for generation after generation." This phrase does not, I think, imply endless punishment.

ing "—seems to state, when rightly *translated* and rightly interpreted, that many shall enjoy the first resurrection, while those who do not shall be doomed to shame and contempt, which (for all that appears in the text) may fall upon them while *dead;* for the word דֵּרָאוֹן here used is applied to "dead corpses" in Is. lxvi. 24. On this text see Mr. White's *Life in Christ,* p. 172. The Jews interpreted the passage of "death and immobility."—Weill, *Le Judaisme,* iv. dogm. xiii. ch. iii. § 1.

Baba Mezia, p. 58.—"All who go down into Gehenna rise up again, with the exception of those who go down and do not rise, the adulterer," &c.[1]

Philippson, in his *Israelitische Religionslehre* (ii. 255), says, when speaking of immortality, "*Die Rabbiner nehmen keine Ewigkeit der Höllenstrafen an*, auch die grössten Sünder werden nur 'Generationen hindurch' gestraft. Allegorisch drucken sie dies auch so aus, dass zwischen der Hölle und dem Paradiese nur ein Zwei Finger breiter Zwischenraum sei, so dass es also dem reinigen Sünder sehr leicht wird aus der ersteren in das letztere zu gelangen." (Midrash, *Kohelet*.)

"With respect to the teachings of the present day, I think it would be safe to say that *they do not teach endless retributive suffering*. They hold that it is not conceivable that a God of Mercy and Justice would ordain infinite punishment for finite wrong-doing."

So writes the Rev. H. N. Adler. "Of this you may be quite sure," wrote the late Dr. Deutsch, with his usual impassioned energy, to the Rev. S. Cox, "that there is *not a word in the Talmud* that lends any support to that damnable dogma of endless torment."

"The upshot is," says Rabbi Marks, "that the Jewish doctors laboured rather to adorn the future of the good, than to adorn the destiny of the wicked. Stronger than their fear of justice is their belief in the Divine mercy. '*He will not contend for ever, neither will He retain His anger to eternity*' (Ps. ciii. 9), which is a power-

---

[1] It appears from other passages of the Talmud that these latter were supposed by some of the Jews to be *annihilated* ; but even this was the *rarer* view, though favoured by Maimonides, Jad Hachazaka, Hilchoth *Teshuba* viii. § 1. Rabbi Adler refers me to *two* Post-Talmudic Rabbis (R. Saadjah and R. J seph Albu, in his *Sepher Ikkarim* iv. 36) who appear to teach endless torments for the few. Hartwig Wessely, the friend of Moses Mendelssohn, wrote a valuable little treatise on Jewish opinion respecting this subject, and there are some remarks in Brecher's *Unsterblichkeitslehre*.

ful argument against the modern Christian doctrine of everlasting woe."

The Chief Rabbi of Avignon, B. Mosse, has written against the doctrine of endless torments in his local journal, *La Famille de Jacob*.

The Chief Rabbi Michel A. Weill, in his elaborate work, *Le Judaïsme, ses Dogmes et sa Mission*, distinctly decides that the doctrine of endless torment is Scripturally untenable. He treats Gehenna not as a real denomination, but as a figurative expression for chastisement. Of the fire and flames he says, " Qui ne reconnaît dans ces termes l'hyperbole prophétique et poétique, qui est comme le génie de la littérature sacrée." He refers to other passages, such as Is. xlviii. 22, lvii. 21, 1 Sam. xxv. 29, &c., to show the spirituality of punishment, while he explains that "they shall no more see'the light," of Ps. xlix. 20, as perhaps identical with the כרת, *kareth*, or "excision" of the Mosaic code. "Would there not," he asks, " be a flagrant contradiction between endless torments and the goodness of God so magnificently celebrated in Biblical annals? Does not Moses announce to us, does he not himself invoke in solemn circumstances 'the Lord, the Lord God, merciful and gracious, long-suffering and abundant in goodness and truth, keeping mercy for thousands, forgiving iniquity, transgression, and sin' (Ex. xxxiv. 6, 7)? Does not the prophet say, in the name of the Lord, 'I will not contend for ever, neither will I be always wroth, for the spirit would fail before me and the souls that I have made' (Is. lvii. 16)? And the Psalmist of Israel, how does he speak on this subject? 'His wrath endureth but the twinkling of an eye, but His favour a lifetime ' (Ps. xxx. 5). *Nothing, therefore, seems more incompatible with the true Biblical tradition than an eternity of suffering and chastisement."* [1]

[1] *Le Judaïsme*, iv. p. 590.

P

But while it is interesting to find this unanimity of opinion in a matter of simple exegesis among modern Rabbis, it is to the Mishna that we should look for the nearest approach to the Jewish view of Gehenna in the time of our Lord. Now according to Dr. Dewes,[1] Gehenna is alluded to four or five times only in the Mishna, and from these passages we learn that "the judgment of Gehenna is for twelve months," that "*it shall fail*" though they who go into it shall not fail," and that "Gehenna is nothing but a day in which the impious shall be burnt." Even Bartolocci, after fifty-six quarto pages on Gehenna, is obliged to confess that the Jews "did not believe in a material fire, and thought that such fire as they did believe in would one day be put out."

Just as in the middle ages we have the most pitiless and the most material picture of hell, so it is in the dark and evil days in which the Pirke R. Eleazar and the Zohar were written that we find the most intimidating pictures of Gehenna. But so incontestable an authority as the great Rabbi Akiba, the second Moses, the second Ezra of the oral law, said, "*The duration of the punishment of the wicked in Gehenna is twelve months*" (Adyoth, ii. 10). He quotes Is. lxvi. 23 in this sense. This indeed was the prevalent conception.[2] Some Rabbis said Gehenna only lasted from Passover to Pentecost. Even in Zohar (in *Genes. col.* 205) it is said that Noah stayed *twelve months* in the Ark because the judgment of sinners lasts so long, and Rabbis Jose, Jehuda, and Eliezer are quoted in favour of this view (Buxtorf, *Lex. Talm. s. v.* םﬥﬣﬡ). The figurative nature of our Lord's language finds striking illustration in such passages as "Better put thyself in a fiery oven than make thy neighbour blush in public" (Berachoth, *f.* 43, 2).

---

[1] *Plea for Rational Translation*, p. 23.

[2] See Eisenmenger, *Entd. Judenth.* p. 354. Rabbi argued "It is absurd to say that the (morally) dead will live, seeing that even in life they are dead."

Even the few Rabbis who held another opinion were far more merciful in their interpretation than modern Christians. They held that the least repentance, even the slightest velleity of repentance, was an impenetrable shield against retribution, even at the moment of death ;[1] and the due performance of even a single precept of the law entitled a man to the future world (*olum ha-ba*).[2] They interpreted Job xxxiii. 23 in the sense that 999 hostile testimonies before God were outweighed by one favourable testimony.[3] They thus hold the salvation of the vast majority of men, and reduce almost to zero the number of those whose doom they regard as final – those only who have not done one meritorious act, or had one desire to repent. "So that, *even taken lit-rally*," says Chief Rabbi Weill, "endless torment loses its terror, since it does not involve conceptions which militate against a merciful God, whose loving-kindness is over all His works."

R. Saadja, in his *Sepher ha-emunah*, does, indeed, hold the doctrine of endless torment, but holds that even without repentance the majority of mankind are admitted into grace if they have not committed capital crimes. If their good deeds preponderate over their evil, the sorrows of earth are sufficient to present them pure to heaven. In fact, Saadja extends so widely the range of penitence, and diminishes so greatly the numbers of the doomed, that he brightens his own horizon after making it seem dark.

If any Rabbi may be regarded as specially entitled to explain the views of the Jews, it is surely Moses Maimonides, "the eagle of the doctors," of whom the Jews say "that from Moses to Moses there was no one like Moses."[4] In his *Yad Hachazaka* he makes the

---

[1] See the singular tenderness and leniency of the views of Maimonides. *Yad Hachazakah*, I. vii.

[2] Sanhedrin, p. 111; Maccoth, *ad fin.*; Ikkarim, iv. 29.

[3] Shabbath, p. 32.   [4] ממשה ועד משה לא קם כמשה·

future life immaterial, and says that the worst of all punishments is *Kareth*, "excision," which he explains as *annihilation* (Num. xv. 31), and says that it is allegorically described by the prophets as *Abaddon, Tophet,* and "the horseleach, expressions of destruction and corruption, in consequence of there being that destruction after which there is no existence, and that ruin which admits of no reparation."[1] He makes Gehenna a *name* or metaphor, explained by some of *the sun,* by others of an inward fire (of remorse).[2]

Maimonides' opinion as to the annihilation of the wicked is doubtless derived from the famous passage of the Talmud (Rosh Hashanak, 17), which says that after twelve months of expiation the bodies of the wicked cease to exist, their soul is burned, and a wind scatters their cinders under the feet of the just."

Rabbi Bar Nachman regards this passage as so metaphorical that he interprets it as a quietude after Gehenna, *a relative beatitude* inferior to that of the just. It is only for a few atheists and renegades that he reserves a more terrible *kareth.* But even in these cases he finds it impossible to get over the distinct statement of the Talmud, "*After the last judgment Gehenna exists no longer.*"[3] "The future world," he says, "the *olam haba,* will have its Gehenna, but the last times (*Leadoth labo*) will have it no more."

R. Albo[4] is another of the few Rabbis who admit endless torment—if indeed these few really do mean endlessness by the expressions which they use. He ranks future retribution under

<hr/>

[1] *Yad Hachazakah Hilchoth Teshuba,* viii. § 1. See Surenhusius Mishna, vi. 265.

[2] Mal. iv. 1, 2; Abhoda Zara; Is. xxx. 11; Bereshith Rabba, 6; Weill, iv. 606.

[3] Nedarin, 8; Midrash Rabba, 1, § 30; Aboda Zara. 3 (Resh Lakish).

[4] *Ikkarim,* iv. 30—40.

three grades: (1) Gehenna for a year, and then blessedness; (2) Gehenna for a year, and then annihilation; (3) "Eternal" chastisement for a few renegades, &c. Yet he dwells on the boundless mercy of God, and founds the remission of eternal punishment, for all except the worst, on Ps. lxii. 14, Micah vii. 18—20, &c.

It will be seen, therefore, that even the few exceptional Rabbis who diverged into this view held it in a form unspeakably less repellent than modern writers; and that their Gehenna was far more like Purgatory than Hell. And in arriving at this conclusion they can barely reconcile it with the more ancient authority of the Mishna and Gemara.

Further, the Rabbis, like all Romanist theologians, held that "nothing can resist repentance." In the *Midrash on Koheleth* the answer to the question, "Why did God create Paradise and Gehenna," we read, "In order that the one may save from the other." But what is the distance between them? According to Johanam, a wall; according to Acha, a palm; according to other Rabbis, *only a finger* (see Eisenmenger, pp. 314, 315). And the inference drawn is that even from Gehenna the guilty can be redeemed by a return to duty.

Generally, it may be stated with confidence that the Rabbinic opinion was that of Abarbanel,[1] that the soul would only be punished in Gehenna for a time proportionate to the extent of its faults; and it is in accordance with this belief, and that in annihilation as being "the second death," that we must interpret the passages which are sometimes adduced from the Targums of Jonathan and Onkelos and from various parts of the Book of Enoch.[2] I have not referred to the vague testimony of Josephus,[3] because I regard him as an

---

[1] *Miphaloth Elohim,* viii. 6.
[2] See Gfrörer, *Jahrb. des Heils,* ii. 289, 311.
[3] *Ant.* xviii. 3, *B. J.* ii. 8. See Ewald, *Gesch.* v. 366 (E. Tr.)

utterly untrustworthy witness, and because what he says is contradicted on this as on a multitude of other subjects by overwhelming
and untainted testimony.

4. Now will honest, serious, and competent readers weigh the
plain literal meaning of the texts which follow—the number of
which might easily be trebled —and in weighing them with an earnest
and prayerful desire to get rid of traditional bias and attain to
truth, will they also do as follows ?—

i. Examine their own reason and conscience as to all that they
know, and all that the Bible teaches, respecting the love of God, and
redemption through Jesus Christ.

ii. See *how very little*, which is in the least degree decisive, they
can produce on the other side ; and how for every word of that
very little an explanation is offered, demonstrably tenable, and far
more in accordance with history than that which they adopt.

iii. Consider the tremendous weight of evidence which must be
thrown against their private interpretation from the fact that neither
the Jewish nor the Christian Church has ever been able dogmatically
to sanction it.

iv. Remember that in the extreme form in which they hold it,
which excludes anything resembling Purgatory, it is directly opposed
to a large body of primitive teaching, and to the views of the entire
Roman Church.

v. Give due weight to the fact that many who have devoted years
of earnest labour to the inquiry—ripe scholars and good men, orthodox Fathers, eminent theologians, profound thinkers, holy and
reverent inquirers—have come to the deliberate conclusion that there
is not a single text in all Scripture which necessitates a belief in
endless torment.

vi. Bear specially in mind that it rests, almost if not quite *exclusively*,
on the meanings which they attach to two words, "Gehenna" and

" Æonian " : of which the first, interpreted by the only possible means of interpretation open to us, *cannot* bear the sense which they attribute to it ; and the other is over and over again applied in Scripture to indefinite but limited time, or to that which transcends all conception of time.[1]

vii. Be shamed into a little humility—a little doubt as to their own absolute infallibility on all religious subjects—a little sense of their possible ignorance or invincible prejudice—a little abstinence from cheap anathemas and contemptible calumnies—a little avoidance of such base weapons of controversy as the assertion that those who hold such views as I here have advocated are repeating the devil's whisper, " Thou shalt not surely die "[2]—by not losing sight of the fact that (1) these views have been held in substance, not only (as I have said) by great teachers and holy saints, but also by whole Churches ; and (2) that they are theoretically involved in practices so universal and so primitive as prayers for the dead. The *Kaddish*, or prayer for the dead, in the Jewish liturgies is probably as old as the time of our Lord, and if so was by Him unreproved, though it was believed to be efficacious for the relief of souls in Gehenna. Eminent commentators, comparing 2 Tim. i. 16 and 19, and iv. 19 have believed that St. Paul's prayer for Onesiphorus is a prayer for one who was dead ; and he does not reprove the *principle* of even so superstitious a practice as *baptism* for the dead.[3]

---

[1] I will add one more testimony to the many already adduced. " In Hebrew and Greek the words rendered ' *everlasting* ' have not this sense. They signify ' a long duration of time,' ' a period,' whence the phrase ' during these eternities and beyond ' " ' (De Lammenais).

[2] The same crude charge might be brought with ten thousandfold more force against the doctrine of repentance. It is one of the many signs that in all generations religious bigotry and ignorance repeat themselves, that the very same taunt was aimed at the merciful hopes of Archbishop Tillotson.

[3] 1 Cor. xv. 29.

The ancientness of belief in the validity of prayers for the dead—
"antiquissimâ omnium Ecclesiarum traditione stabilitum" — is
beyond possibility of dispute.[1]   Of the practice itself I give
no opinion ; but it proves most absolutely that the Early Church held
as a certain belief the main point for which I have here contended—
which is, in brief, a possible hope beyond the grave.   When Aerius
taught the modern popular doctrine, "assuming one broad line
of demarcation in the unseen world," he was treated as opposing
the practice of the Church from the beginning [2] (Epiphan. *Hæres.*
75) ; and St. Augustine—whose views (as I have pointed out) were
so far less frightful in many respects than those now prevalent—
distinctly declares that we may pray for the dead, "ut sit plena
remissio, aut certe ut fiat tolerabilior damnatio." [3]

viii. Let them weigh the fact that what Christ did once—namely
preach to the lost, and open for them the prison doors—He may do
again and ever.   The text on which I preached " throws blessed
light on one of the darkest enigmas of Divine Justice—the cases in
which the final doom seems infinitely out of proportion to the lapse
that has incurred it."   This was the interpretation of the early
Fathers. "May not these inspired words of Peter," says Canon
Spence, "hint to us that our Lord's redemptive work is far more
extensive than men usually conceive?"   (Col. i. 20, Eph. i. 10).[4]

If any candid truth-seeker will thus inquire, I have very little
doubt as to the conclusion at which he will arrive.   He will see
that while we most heartily agree with him in admitting the immense
importance attributed by all Scripture to life as a period of probation,
and the certainty that future retribution will be proportionate to the

---

[1] It is needless to point in proof of this to the evidence of the Catacombs as
well as the early Fathers.

[2] *Dict. of Christ. Biog.*, Art. " Death."

[3] *Enchir.* 110.   [4] *Bibl. Educator,* i. 118.

willingness and heinousness of our earthly sins, neither Scripture, nor the Church, nor anything that we learn from any source within or without us respecting God, in any way sanctions the popular dogma of an irreversible doom at the moment of death, for all who die impenitent, to endless physical or mental torment. Of the opposite view,—the restitution in its most literal sense of all things,—the brightest and ablest of the Scotch prelates, Bishop Ewing of Argyll and the Isles, said in language which goes farther than I can go, "Unless this be held as a matter of faith and not as a speculative dogma, it is practically valueless. With me this final victory is not a matter of speculation at all, but of positive faith ; and *to disbelieve it would be for me to cease altogether either to trust or to worship God.*"

Lastly, I do not for a moment mean to offer the following catena of texts as even approximately complete. To adduce all the passages which deepen in my mind the trust in Eternal Hope would be to transcribe one half of the Scriptures. Rarely do I read the daily Psalms or the daily lessons without meeting with expressions which seem to run directly counter to the common doctrine. It is also a most important consideration that we must judge from the silence of Scripture as well as from its utterances. Were there any truth, in the numberless accretions which have gathered round this simple nucleus that there is a retribution for sin beyond the grave, surely they are of such momentous importance that they would not have been left in an obscurity so deep that the Church has never been able to sanction them, though she was well aware that some of her truest sons have openly rejected them. The silence of St. Paul as to any such doctrines in such passages as Rom. ii. 8, 9 ; v. 21, vi. 23 ; Gal. v. 21, vi. 8; Phil. iii. 18, 19 ;—the reticence of St. John in such passages as 1 John iii. 14, 15, v. 16—in all which places the nature of the subjects handled would have led the Apostles to make explicit mention of endless torment, had they embraced any such belief —cannot by any possibility be the result of accident.[1] "That the doctrinal writings of these three chief teachers of the Gospel—St. Paul, St. Peter, and St. John—are wholly destitute of any assertion of the endless misery of sinners as the literal sense," says Mr. White, "can be verified by every reader."[2] Even Luther, like almost every great and true-hearted teacher on this subject, while constantly maintaining the doctrine of endless torment in nearly its present form, yet slides unconsciously into more hopeful expressions ; "God forbid," he says, "*that I should limit the time for acquiring faith to the present life! In the depths of the divine mercy* there may be opportunity to win it in the *future state.*"[3]

---

[1] See essays on Eternal Death by Mr. Barlow, Fellow of Trin. Coll Dublin. "There is not one place of Scripture which occurs to me," said Dr. Isaac Watts, 'where the word death . . . necessarily signifies a certain miserable immortality of the soul."

[2] *Life in Christ*, p. 347.

[3] Letter to Hansen von Rechenberg, 1522. (Alger, *Doctrine of a Future Life*, p. 421. To the Rabbinic passages already quoted may be added the following : *Zijoni, f.* 69, 3, "only a thread's thickness between Paradise and Gehenna ;" *Asarath Maamaroth, f.* 85, 1, "there will hereafter be no Gehenna ;" *Jalkuth Shimoni, f.* 46, 1, "Gabriel and Michael will open the 8,000 gates of Gehenna and let out Israelites and righteous Gentiles ;" *Jalkuth Chadash, f.* 57, 1, "the righteous bring out of Gehenna imperfect souls ;" *Jalkuth Rubeni, f.* 167, 4, "Sabbaths and *refrigeria* of the doomed ;" *Zohar in Exod. Tr. Gibborim, f.* 70, 1 ; *Nishmath Chajim, f.* 83, 1 ; *Jalkuth Shimoni, f.* 88, 3, and many other passages speak of *twelve months* as the period of punishment in Gehenna. In a magnificent passage of *Othoth* (attributed to R. Akiba) it is said that God has a key of Gehenna, and that He will preach to all the righteous : that Zerubbabel shall say the *Kaddish* and an *Amen!* shall sound forth from Gehenna, and that Gabriel and Michael will open the 40,000 gates of Gehenna and set free the damned. Akiba founds this on Is. xxvi. 2, reading *Shomer Amenim*, "observing the Amen," for *Shomer Emunim*, "keeping the truth." Lastly, in *Emek Hammelech, f.* 138, 4, "the wicked stay in Gehenna till the resurrection, and then the Messiah, passing through it, redeems them." These and other passages are collected in Stephelin's *Rabbinical Literature* (1748), ii. 31-71.

These then are some of the texts to be considered. The comments which I have quoted must be understood with such limitations as I have previously indicated.

Gen. iii. 15. "And I will put enmity between thee and the woman, and between thy seed and her seed ; it shall bruise thy head, and thou shalt bruise his heel."[1]

Gen. xii. 3. " And in thy seed shall all families of the earth be blessed." See also Gen. xxii. 18, Gal. iii. 8, Acts. iii. 25.[2]

Ps. ciii. 9. "He will not alway be chiding : neither keepeth He His anger for ever." See the Psalms *passim*, and Mic. vii. 18. "He retaineth not His anger for ever, because He delighted in mercy."

Ps. cxxxix. 8. "If I make my bed in hell, behold, Thou art there."[3]

---

[1] "How could this be so, if Satan triumphed by gaining millions to be his slaves? In this case could it be said, as in Is. liii. 13, 'He shall see of the travail of his soul and be satisfied, for he shall bear their iniquities'?" Dr. Chauncey, *The Mystery hid from all ages, or the Salvation of all Men.*—1784.

[2] Yet Du Moulin (*Reflections on the Number of the Elect*, 1622) affirms that not one in a million from Adam downwards shall be saved.

[3] " What hell may be I know not : this I know
I cannot lose the presence of the Lord :
One arm—Humility—takes hold upon
His dear humanity ; the other, Love,
Clasps His divinity, so where I go
He goes ; and better fire-walled hell with Him,
Than golden-gated Paradise without."

Isaiah lvii. 16. " For I will not contend for ever, neither will I be always wroth : for the spirit should fail before Me, and the souls which I have made."

Isaiah xlix. 9. " That thou mayest say to the prisoners, Go forth ; to them that are in darkness, Shew yourselves." [1]

Hos. vi. 1. " Come, and let us return unto the Lord : for He hath torn, and He will heal us ; He hath smitten, and He will bind us up."

Hos. xiv. 4. " I will heal their backsliding, I will love them freely ; for mine anger is turned away from him."

John i. 29. " Behold the Lamb of God, which taketh away the sin of the world."

John iii. 17. " God sent not His Son into the world to con- demn the world ; but that the world through Him might be saved." [2]

John iii. 35. " The Father loveth the Son, and hath given all things into His hand." (c. 42, and 1 John iv. 14, " The Saviour of the Universe.") [3]

John xii. 32. " And I, if I be lifted up from the earth, will draw all men (but *leg. πάντα*) unto me." See also Luke ix. 56, |__

---

[1] Is. xxxiii. 14, and other passages sometimes quoted to prove endless torment, have not the very remotest connection with the subject. And the fact that in Mark ix. 50, our Lord is borrowing the purely temporal language of Is. lxvi. 24, is, even alone, an argument of overwhelming force against the meaning which has been attached to His expressions.

[2] What affinity is there between these utterances and such a sentence as this from Calvin ? " Unde factum est, ut *tot gentes una cum liberis eorum infanti- bus aeternâ morte involveret lapsus Adae abseque remedio,* nisi quia Deo ita visum est? *Decretum horribile fateor* " (*Instit.* iii. 23, 7).

[3] " The happiness of the blest rests, not on a word or syllable, but on their perfect union with God ; we have *no data whatever* on which to ground the assertion that the eternity of evil is equally unlimited, absolute, and infinite." Rev Archer Gurney.

"For the Son of Man is not come to destroy men's lives, but to save them."

John xv. 22. "He that knew not his Lord's will and did commit things worthy of stripes *shall be beaten with few stripes.*"

1 John ii. 2. "He is the propitiation for our sins, and not for ours only, but also περὶ ὅλου τοῦ κόσμου."

Acts. iii. 21. "Whom the heaven must receive until the times of restitution of all things (ἀποκαταστάσεως πάντων), which God hath spoken by the mouth of all His holy prophets since the world began."

Eph. i. 10. "That in the dispensation of the fulness of times He might gather together in one all things in Christ, both which are in heaven, and which are on earth."[1]

Phil. ii. 10, 11. "That at the name of Jesus every knee should bow, of things in heaven, and things in earth, and things under the earth."[2]

Col. i. 19, 20. "For it hath pleased the Father that in him should all fulness dwell ; and, having made peace through the blood of His cross, by Him to reconcile all things unto Himself (ἀποκαταλλάξαι τὰ πάντα εἰς αὐτὸν εἰρηνοποιήσας, κ. τ. λ.) ; by Him, I say, whether they be things in earth, or things in heaven." See also Rom. viii. 19, 24. "For the earnest expectation of the creature waiteth for the manifestation of the sons of God. For

---

[1] "Will any one contend that the Pauline conception would be satisfied by the endless existence of the majority of the human race in misery and sin? Has Christ subdued those who gnash their teeth at Him because He makes them suffer? Is this the working whereby He is able to subdue even all things unto Himself? Will God be *all in all* when vast multitudes of His creatures are in impotent but absolute rebellion against Him?" Rev. J. Ll. Davies, *Manifestation of the Sons of God,* p. 358.

[2] "Every number of destroyed sinners . . . . must through the all-working, all-redeeming love of God, which never ceaseth, come at last, to know that they had lost, and have found again such a God of Love as this." William Law.

the creature was made subject unto vanity, not willingly, but by reason of Him who hath subjected the same in hope, because the creature itself also shall be delivered from the bondage of corruption into the glorious liberty of the children of God. For we are saved by hope."

Rom. v. 15. "For if through the offence of one many (οἱ πολλοί) be dead, much more the grace of God, and the gift by grace, which is by one man, Jesus Christ, hath abounded unto many (τοὺς πολλούς)"; and verse 17 and verse 18. "Therefore as by the offence of one judgment came upon all men to condemnation; even so by the righteousness of one the free gift came upon all men unto justification of life;" and verses 20, 21. "But where sin abounded, grace did much more abound: that as sin hath reigned unto death, even so might grace reign through righteousness unto eternal life by Jesus Christ our Lord."

Rom. xi. 32. "For God hath concluded them all in unbelief, that He might have mercy upon all."

Rom. xiv. 9. "For to this end Christ both died, and rose, and revived, that He might be Lord both of the dead and living."

1 Cor. xv. 22. "For as in Adam all die, even so in Christ shall all be made alive;" and verses 24—28. "Then cometh the end, when He shall have delivered up the kingdom to God, even the Father; when He shall have put down all rule and all authority and power. For He must reign, till He hath put all enemies under His feet. The last enemy that shall be destroyed is death. For He hath put all things under His feet.[1] But when He saith all things are put under Him, it is manifest that He is excepted, which did put all things under Him. And when all

---

[1] "If all things without exception shall be subjected to Christ, then death, the *second* death as well as the *first* death, will be finally swallowed up in victory." Dr. Chauncey.

things shall be subdued unto Him, then shall the Son also Himself be subject unto Him that put all things under Him, that God may be all in all (τὰ πάντα ἐν πᾶσιν)." [1]

2 Cor. v. 19. "To wit, that God was in Christ, reconciling the world unto Himself, not imputing their trespasses unto them ; and hath committed unto us the word of reconciliation." [2]

1 Tim. ii. 4. [3] "Who willeth (θέλει) all men to be saved and to come to the knowledge of the truth" (Cf. v. 6).

1 Tim. iv. 10. "For therefore we both labour and suffer reproach, because we trust in the living God, who is the Saviour of all men, specially of those that believe ; " and ii. 1-6, esp. 6, "Who gave Himself a ransom for all, to be testified in due time (ὁ δοὺς ἑαυτὸν ἀντίλυτρον ὑπὲρ πάντων· τὸ μαρτύριον καιροῖς ἰδίοις)."

Tit. ii. 11, 12. Not as in English version, but, "For the grace of God hath appeared, which is saving to all men (ἡ σωτήριος πᾶσιν ἀνθρώποις)." [4]

---

[1] "*Ut sit Deus omnia in omnibus.* Significatur hic novum quiddam sed idem summum et perenne, omnia (*adeoque omnes*), sine ullâ interpellatione, nullâ creaturâ obstantè, nullo hoste obturbante, erunt subordinata Filio, Filius Patri. H c τέλος est, h.c finis, et apex. Ultra ne Apostolus quidem quo eat habet . . . Ab impiis in mundo habetur Deus pro nihilo, et apud sanctos multa obstant ne sit unus omnia apud ipsos, sed tum erit *Omnia in omnibus.*" Bengel, *Gnomon*, p. 760.

[2] "The sacrifice for sin was infinitely more potent for good, than sin for evil." Rev. E. S. Ffoulkes.

[3] On the vain attempts of St. Augustine and Calvin to do away with the force of this statement, see Gieseler, *Eccl. Hist.* i, 383 (E. Tr.)

[4] "The sacred writers are singularly emphatical in expressing their truth. They could not have been more full and peremptory, had they intended to guard against men's straining their words to another meaning. They speak n t only of 'Christ's dying for us,' 'for our sins,' 'for sinners,' 'for the ungodly,' 'for the unjust,' but affirm, in yet more extensive terms, that He died 'for the world,' 'for the whole world,' yes, that they might not be misunderstood they say that 'God laid on Him the iniquity of us all ; ' yes, that ' He tasted death for every man ; ' yes, that ' He gave His life a ransom for all.' " Dr. Chauncey.

Heb. ii. 14. "Forasmuch, then, as the children are partakers of flesh and blood, He also Himself likewise took part of the same; that through death He might destroy him that had the power of death, that is, the devil;" and verses 8, 9, "Thou hast put all things in subjection under His feet. For in that He put all in subjection under Him, He left nothing that is not put under Him. But now we see not yet all things put under Him. But we see Jesus, who was made a little lower than the angels for the suffering of death, crowned with glory and honour; that He by the grace of God (or rather χωρὶς θεοῦ) '*for every rational being, or for everything (neut.) except God*') should taste death."

Rev. v. 13. "And every creature which is in heaven, and on the earth, and under the earth (ὑποκάτω τῆς γῆς), and such as are in the sea, and all that are in them, heard I saying, Blessing, and honour, and glory, and power, be unto Him that sitteth upon the throne, and unto the Lamb for ever and ever."

Rev. xxi. 4, 5. "And God shall wipe away all tears from their eyes; and there shall be no more death, neither sorrow, nor crying, neither shall there be any more pain : for the former things are passed away. And He that sat upon the throne said, Behold, I make all things new. And He said unto me, Write : for these words are true and faithful."

Rev. xxii. 3. "And there shall be no more curse ;" and see, too, Rev. xx. 14. "And death and hell were cast into the lake of fire."

On all these passages of St. Paul, St. John, and other sacred writers, so strongly and indisputably asserting the doctrine of universal redemption, I will only remark that "*all*" cannot possibly mean, as St. Augustine vainly tries to make out, "omnes prædestinati" (*De Corrept.* 14), or "homines omnis generis" (*Enchir.* 103), or indeed anything except what they say, viz., that Christ died *for all*.

It is, indeed, true that universal *redemption* does not necessarily imply universal *salvation :* but I ask any honest and unbiassed thinker whether the predicted triumph of Christ's cross, and the universality of His future kingdom, are consistent with the popular doctrine that only the few are saved? Bishop Martensen thought that alike universal restoration and never-ending torments were unequivocally taught in Scripture, and that therefore in Scripture, as in life, there were insoluble antinomies. Bishop Thirlwall seems to have inclined to a similar view. My own view is different. It seems to me that if many passages of Scripture be taken *quite literally*, universal restoration is unequivocally taught, just as, if many passages be taken quite literally, the final annihilation of the wicked is taught ; but that *endless torments are nowhere clearly taught*—the passages which appear to teach that doctrine being either obviously figurative or historically misunderstood. If the decision be made to turn *solely on the literal* meaning of Scripture, I have no hesitation whatever in declaring my strong conviction that the universalist and annihilist theories have far more evidence of this sort for them than the popular view. It may be asked, Why then am I unable to adopt the universalist opinion? The answer is simple. It is because one or two passages —though far more than their due significance seems to have been attributed to them—seem to make it unwise to speak dogmatically on a matter which God has not clearly revealed. Comparing Scripture with Scripture limiting Scripture by Scripture, and judging of Scripture—as we are encouraged and taught to do—by that spirit of man, which is the candle of the Lord, I see no tenable view but that ancient and noble one which I have here tried-—alas ! very imperfectly, but to the best of my power under present circumstances —to set forth, and to defend.

Q

www.ingramcontent.com/pod-product-compliance
Lightning Source LLC
Chambersburg PA
CBHW021048030726
47496CB00006B/1740